Thematic Unit

Immigration

D0131655

Written by Patricia Sima, Sharon Coan, Ina Massler Levin, and Karen Goldfluss

Illustrated by Cheryl Buhler, Sue Fullam, Keith Vasconcelles, Sandy Welch, and Theresa Wright

The authors wish to acknowledge the contributions of Judy Vaden.

Teacher Created Materials, Inc.
P.O. Box 1040
Huntington Beach, CA 92647
©1993 Teacher Created Materials, Inc.
Made in U.S.A.

ISBN-1-55734-234-4

Table of Contents

Introduction

Immigration contains a captivating whole language, thematic unit. Its 80 exciting pages are filled with a wide variety of lesson ideas and reproducible pages designed for use with intermediate children. At its core are four high-quality children's literature selections: *Do People Grow on Family Trees?*, *Molly's Pilgrim, How Many Days To America?*, and *Hello, My Name Is Scrambled Eggs*. For each of these books activities are included which set the stage for reading, encourage the enjoyment of the book, and extend the concepts gained. In addition, the theme is connected to the curriculum with activities in language arts, math, science, social studies, art, music, and life skills. Many of these activities encourage cooperative learning. Suggestions and patterns for a bulletin board are provided for the busy teacher. Furthermore, a culminating activity that allows students to synthesize their knowledge in order to produce products that can be shared beyond the classroom completes this valuable teacher resource.

This thematic unit includes the following:

❑ **Literature selections**—summaries of four children's books with related lessons (complete with reproducible pages) that cross the curriculum

❑ **Planning guides**—daily suggestions for sequencing lessons

❑ **Writing ideas**—writing suggestions that cross the curriculum

❑ **Homework suggestions**—extending the unit to the child's home and helping students to prepare for the reading of the books

❑ **Curriculum connections**—in language arts, math, science, art, social studies, and life skills

❑ **Group projects**—to foster cooperative learning

❑ **A culminating activity**—which requires students to synthesize their learning to produce a product or engage in an activity that can be shared with others

❑ **A bibliography**—suggesting additional literature and nonfiction books on the theme

> To keep this valuable resource intact so it can be used year after year, you may wish to punch holes in the pages and store them in a three-ring binder.

Do People Grow on Family Trees? Genealogy for Kids and Other Beginners

by Ira Wolfman

Summary

This book serves two purposes: It provides the motivation and suggests the means for people to research their family histories. And it provides a chronicle of immigration to America, throughout its history including the earliest Native Americans, the Pilgrims, the African slaves, the Eastern and Western Europeans, the Asians and the peoples from other North and South American countries. It shares the reasons why and the means by which people from all over the world came to America including those who were forced to come as slaves. Its focus, however, is on Ellis Island through which at least one ancestor of four out of every ten Americans passed. (All four of the author's grandparents came to America by way of Ellis Island.) A foreward by Alex Haley endorses the author's premise that children can never start too early to collect their families' histories and stories.

The outline below is a suggested plan for using the various activities that are presented in this unit. Adapt these ideas to fit your classroom situation.

Sample Plan

Lesson One
- Display bulletin board (page 77) and introduce unit.
- Read and discuss Foreward.
- Read and discuss Introduction. (page 6)
- Prepare and decorate folder or booklet for collection of family history. (page 12)
- Write letters to relatives requesting help for unit. (See page 11 for sample.)

Lesson Two
- Read Chapter One. (See suggested activities, page 6.)
- Begin collecting family stories.
- Begin collecting information for family tree. (page 13)
- Use math activity, page 6, Chapter 1, #3

Lesson Three *(May take more than one day.)*
- Read Chapter Two. (See suggested activities, pages 6-8.)
- Write letters to appropriate sources for information on immigration.

- Begin research on historical events to find their impact on immigration. (page 14)
- Study and compare slavery and indentured servitude in early America.
- Make immigration maps and graphs. (pages 56-58)

Lesson Four
- Read Chapter Three. (See suggested activities, page 8.)
- Begin interviews with family members.
- Use pages 16-17 to help students organize and plan to share their family histories.

Lesson Five *(May take more than one day.)*
- Read Chapter Four. (See suggested activities, pages 8-9.)
- Create an immigrant's diary. (page 18)
- Write about what to bring when moving from one location to another. (page 8, #4)
- Study Ellis Island and do an Ellis Island simulation. (page 62)
- Use chapter photos as story starters. (pages 53-55)

Sample Plan *(cont.)*

Lesson Six *(Will take more than one day.)*
- Use the activities for *Molly's Pilgrim* and *How Many Days to America?* (pages 19-30)

Lesson Seven
- Read Chapter Five. (See suggested activities, page 9)
- Collect family artifacts.
- Collect family recipes. Make a class cookbook. (See page 73 for examples.)

Lesson Eight
- Read Chapter Six. (See suggested activities, pages 9-10)
- Do a map activity to record where immigrants settled.
- Research why people of an ethnic group tend to settle near others from their own country.
- Find a metaphor to describe America's ethnic diversity.

Lesson Nine *(Will take more than one day.)*
- Do activities for *Hello, My Name Is Scrambled Eggs.* (pages 31-45)

Lesson Ten
- Read Chapter Seven. (See suggested activities, page 10)
- Research where your class' names come from.
- Make up character names and write a story.

Lesson Eleven *(May take more than one day.)*
- Read Chapter Ten. (See suggested activities, page 10)
- Complete family history books.
- Plan for and hold A Heritage Thanksgiving Festival. (pages 75-76)

Overview of Activities

Setting the Stage

1. Prepare a bulletin board with a large world map that has the Western Hemisphere in the middle. Title it "Where Is Your Family From?" Directions and patterns for completing the bulletin board may be found on pages 77-78.

2. Identify Alex Haley as a famous African-American author who became very involved in finding out about his family background. His discoveries led him to write a book, *Roots*, which was turned into a TV mini-series and had one of the largest audiences in television history. Read and discuss Haley's Forward to *Do People Grow on Family Trees?*

3. Read Ira Wolfman's introduction, "How I Became an Ancestor Detector." Then do some or all of the activities suggested under Introduction from the Chapter by Chapter Activities on page 6.

Enjoying the Book

1. Read the book a chapter at a time and complete selected activities for each chapter from the suggestion on pages 6 to 10.

2. Introduce and review the vocabulary found in the Word Bank on page 46 as it is needed for understanding the book.

Extending the Book

1. Use the children's literature selections and activities (pages 19-45) to provide another look at the immigrant experience.

2. Plan for and carry out the culminating activity, found on pages 75-76.

3. Use the activities suggested for Chapter Ten on page 10.

Chapter by Chapter Activities

Introduction: "How I Became an Ancestor Detector"

1. Read the introduction to introduce the term genealogy. Have students write a letter to their parents asking for help in collecting their family histories or use the letter on page 11.

2. Have students start the folder or notebook they will use to collect their family histories. The cover on page 12 may be used for this project.

Chapter One: "Where You Came From"

1. After reading the three stories ("A Very Big Bedtime Story," "An Expected Route to History," and "A Phone Call to the Past") of people who have made interesting discoveries in the search for their family histories, assign students to begin collecting family stories. They may wish to audio or video tape the telling of the stories first, then write them identifying the teller. For example, "My Grandpa loves to tell about the time he stole a watermelon from a neighbor's field. He got caught and the neighbor punished him by making him eat so much watermelon he was sick. Now I know why my grandpa doesn't like watermelon!"

2. After reading the sidebox, "Your Many Families," have students identify the four family names of their grandparents. Have them record this information on the form on page 13 for inclusion in their family history books.

3. Read the sidebox, "Buddy, can you spare an ancestor?"

   Use an overhead calculator to do the math or have students try it on individual calculators. [2 (parents) x 2 (parents for each) = 4 (grandparents) x 2 (parents for each) = 8 (great grandparents) x 2 (parents for each) = 16 (great, great grandparents), etc.] Challenge students to compute to the fourth great grandparents, the eighth great grandparents, and more. Do they see a mathematical pattern? Can they find a shortcut? If all the names were written on a chart, how many names would there be at each level? See if students can find a way to graphically display their calculations.

Chapter Two: "How We Got Here"

1. Over fifty million people have immigrated to the United States during the last 200 years. Before reading this chapter, write the large number 50,000,000 for the students to see. Brainstorm a list of reasons people would leave their countries to come to America. Review this list when you have read the chapter to see if it agrees with the reasons given by author. Can the reasons be summed up under a few headings?

   Here is one suggested way to conduct your brainstorming session: List all the students' responses on separate lines on chart paper, one after another. Make no comments and edit only for brevity. When the brainstorm is complete, ask students to see if any of the listings seem to go together and why. Decide if short headings or titles could be devised for groups of listings. Write each heading chosen by students on a separate sheet of chart paper. Cut the original list into strips. Divide the class into small groups and distribute the strips among the groups. As a group, students should decide where their listings should go and then defend their choices to the class. When a class consensus is reached, tape or glue the strips into place.

6

Chapter by Chapter Activities *(cont.)*

Chapter Two: "How We Got Here" *(cont.)*

2. Use the sidebox, "Comings and Goings," to introduce or review the terms emigrant and immigrant.

3. Use the sidebox, "Why they left: Family stories," to encourage students to find at least one person, a relative or other, who is an immigrant and ask him or her for the specific reason(s) he or she came to America. Plan a time for students to share these reasons. Can the reasons be categorized under the headings in the brainstorming chart?

4. Have students create their own ads for immigrants after viewing the section titled, "The First Wave."

5. Use a globe or world map to trace the theorized immigration route of "The First Americans." Then show how by the 1400's Native American tribes populated all of North America. Show again on a map how these tribes were killed off and driven from their land by advancing immigrants from other cultures. Encyclopedias are good sources for this information.

   Write the Bureau of Indian Affairs, 1849 C Street NW, Washington, DC, 20240, for more information on Native Americans.

6. Have students formulate questions to be addressed to the Society of Mayflower Descendants. Write a letter from your class asking these questions and send it to the address found in the sidebox, "Famous early immigrants: The Pilgrims."

7. Assign one of the following topics (or others of your choice) to small groups of students. Have them research it to discover its impact on immigration to America. Groups may use the form on page 14 to organize their information.

Indentured Servants	**The Gold Rush**	**Industrial Revolution**
Homesteading	**Irish Potato Famine**	**Transcontinental Railroad**
The Oregon Trail	**The Great Depression**	**Chinese Exclusion Act**
Immigration Quotas	**World War I**	**World War II**

8. Discuss the words in The Declaration of Independence, "all men are created equal," in light of the fact that women, Native Americans, and African slaves were not treated equally to white males at the time it was written.

9. Do the math to compute the number of immigrants who arrived in the peak year, 1907, at an average of over 3000 a day for every day of that year. Or, divide 1,285,000 by 365 to see how many immigrants arrived per day.

10. On a large map of the United States, use flag pins to mark the ports of entry used by ancestors of the children in your class.

11. Discuss "The Great Migration" of African-Americans within the United States around the time of World War I. What were the reasons for this? How were these reasons the same or different from the reasons people emigrated from other countries? Have students' families moved within the United States? Why? How is this the same and/or different from moving from one country to another country? Discuss the problems associated with a move within a country. Are they the same or different from an immigrant's move? Use the Venn diagram on page 15 to organize the results of this discussion.

Chapter by Chapter Activities (cont.)

Chapter Two: "How We Got Here" (cont.)

12. Compare slavery and indentured servitude. A Venn diagram could also be used to organize this comparison.

13. Have students choose one of the completed Venn diagrams and use it to write a three-paragraph essay. Paragraph One is how the two variables are alike. Paragraph Two is how they are different or contrast. Paragraph Three is an opinion paragraph based on the evidence. For example, "I think it was better to be an indentured servant because..."

14. Use a map and the graphing information on pages 56-58 to locate and record the places and numbers of immigrants who came to the United States at various times.

Chapter Three: "Finding Your Families"

1. Ask students to begin interviewing family members to see where their families fit into America's immigration picture. Have students use the form on page 16 to start recording the information they collect.

2. A simplified Family Group Sheet can be found on page 17. After students complete as many of the forms as they can, have them design an imaginative way to display their family information. See sidebox, "Branching Out: Unusual family trees."

Chapter Four: " Coming to America"

1. Have students turn the narrative of the chapter into a first person diary account of an immigrant's trip. Let them choose the place emigrated from, etc., perhaps based on their own ancestry. See page 18 for a reproducible diary cover and page.

2. Read the sidebox, "Not everyone came to the U.S.A." Assign groups of students to research and report upon immigration to the four Western Hemisphere countries mentioned.

3. If you haven't done so yet, this is a good point to begin to use the bulletin board created in Setting the Stage. (See directions on page 77.)

4. Read the sidebox, "What they brought." Have students do a quick write about which five things (if only five could be taken) they would choose as necessities to bring on a move and what five things they would consider their most precious possessions that they would not want to leave behind. Are the lists the same? Combine the two lists into the five things which would be taken and explain why.

5. Do the math. If about 60,000 immigrants a year became citizens in Los Angeles every year during the 1980's, how many became citizens in that decade?

6. Ellis Island has recently been restored and dedicated as a national park. Find out about the restoration. Write to Statue of Liberty National Monument, Liberty Island, New York, NY, 10040, for information about one of our newest national parks.

7. Why was Ellis Island called, "The Golden Door?" Why "golden'' and why "door"? An excellent book on Ellis Island and immigration in general is *Ellis Island: New Hope in a New Land* by William Jay Jacobs (Charles Scribner's, 1990).

Chapter by Chapter Activities *(cont.)*

Chapter Four: "Coming to America" *(cont.)*

8. Discuss the differences between the way cabin passengers and steerage passengers were treated when they arrived in the United States. Was this fair?

9. After reading "The lamp beside the golden door," study the Statue of Liberty. Pages 51, 52, 59 and 66 will help you do this.

10. Read "Beware of swindlers!" Why were new immigrants so susceptible to crooks? Do similar things happen today to people who are immigrants and even those who are not? This topic can be elaborated upon if you believe there are problems in your area of which children should be aware.

11. Pair students to role play immigration officer and immigrant. Have them develop answers to the modified list of questions found on page 62. The immigration officer will ask questions and record answers and then switch roles to become the immigrant. Students may pretend to be one of their actual ancestors as they plan how to answer the questions.

12. Use pages 54-55 or photocopy pictures of your choice from Chapter Four. (This is legal if done for classroom use only.) Have each student select a picture to use as a story starter.

13. At this point, you may wish to use the activities for *Molly's Pilgrim* and *How Many Days to America?* (pages 19 - 30) to examine further the problems faced by new immigrants.

14. Read the sidebox, "Coming over the border: Neighbors who immigrated." An easy-to-read novel, *The Skirt* by Gary Soto (Delacorte Press, 1992), provides a glimpse of how a Mexican-American family remembers its native country while living in the United States and opens many possibilities for exploring Mexican-American culture. The art activities on pages 67-69 can also be used in conjunction with this sidebox.

Chapter Five : "Exploring the Past"

1. Use this chapter to stimulate students to collect artifacts and oral histories of their families. Encourage them to share as many of these as possible, but be sensitive to the fact that some family "treasures" are too precious to be brought to school. In this case, have students share written descriptions, drawings, or photos of the items.

2. Family recipes are often handed down from generation to generation and are a type of artifact. Have children bring in a recipe reflecting their heritage and compile a class cookbook. Sample ethnic recipes can be found on page 73.

Chapter Six: "Becoming an American"

1. Discuss how it might feel to have just arrived in America. What would you need to know?

2. Use the book, *Hello, My Name Is Scrambled Eggs*. See suggestions for its use on pages 31-45. Be sure to prepare the *Newcomer's Welcome Book*, pages 47-48.

3. Is there an area of your town or city where people of one ethnic group tend to live together? Interview people from that area to find out why. If possible, visit the area to see how the culture of the "old country" has been transported to America. If there is no ethnic area in your town, visit an ethnic restaurant run by persons from the culture.

Chapter by Chapter Activities (cont.)

Chapter Six: "Becoming an American" (cont.)

4. Discuss the metaphor "melting pot." How does this describe the immigrants' adjustment to America? What does it imply will happen to a groups' traditions from the old country? Is there a better metaphor? Some suggested are "salad bowl," "patchwork quilt," and "mosaic." What do these imply? (Each part is an essential contribution to the whole. The whole would not be complete without each part and each part cannot stand alone as representative of the whole.)

5. After reading the sidebox, "Where they settled," use a map of the United States to have students color code areas where great numbers of similar immigrants settled.

Chapter Seven: "The Name Game"

1. After reading the chapter, have students see if they can figure out where their last names come from. Be sure to use the sidebox "What's in a name?" to help students realize that original spellings may have been changed. They may also wish to research the origins of their grandparents' last names.

2. Students may make up names for characters in a story by using one or more of the naming techniques mentioned in the chapter. For example, they could write a fairy tale in which the characters' names reflect their personal characteristics: (e.g., Sir Goodenough; Knight E. Vil; and Dame Heartwarm.)

Chapters Eight & Nine: "The Paper Chase" & "You Could Look it Up"

Use these chapters with your whole class if students and their families have become hooked on genealogical research. Or, let those few students who choose to pursue the matter in greater depth use the information in the chapters on their own.

Chapter Ten: " Sharing the Wealth"

1. This chapter suggests many ways to share family histories. Choose one or more with your class and carry it out as the culminating activity for the unit. Suggestions for a Heritage Thanksgiving similar to a Family Reunion will be found on pages 75-76.

2. Have students complete their Family History Books by including as many of the items mentioned in the "Family Bestsellers" section as possible. These should certainly be displayed at your culminating festival.

Letter

Dear Parents,

We are about to begin a unit on Immigration. This unit will be very meaningful to the students because they will research their own family histories to discover information about the coming of their ancestors to America. During this process your child will ask you many questions and make contact with other relatives to gather information. Your cooperation will assure that this will be one of our most exciting and personally rewarding units this year.

Thank you for your help.

Sincerely,

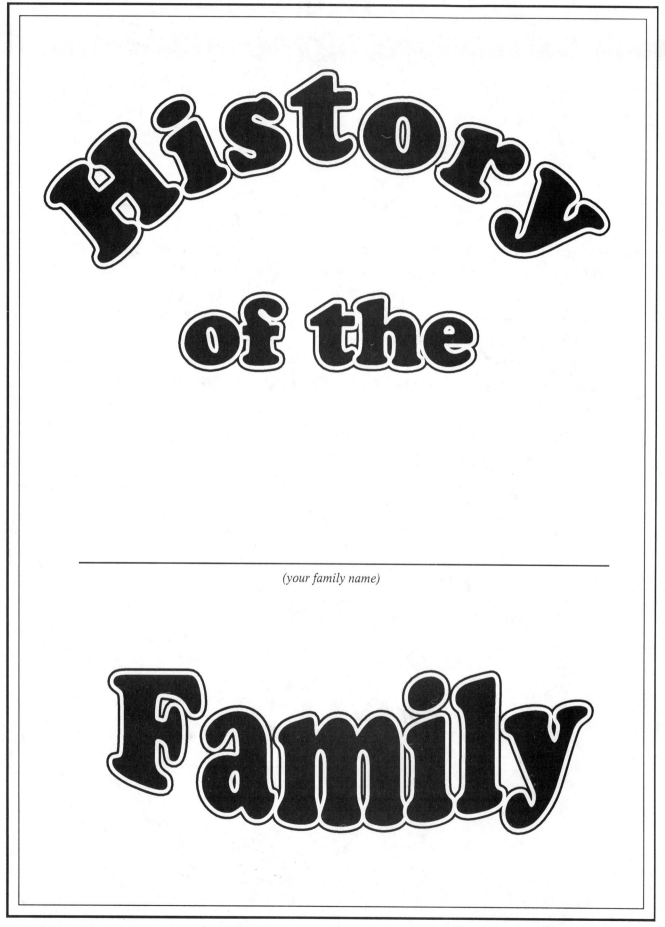

History of the

_____

(your family name)

Family

12

Four of My Families

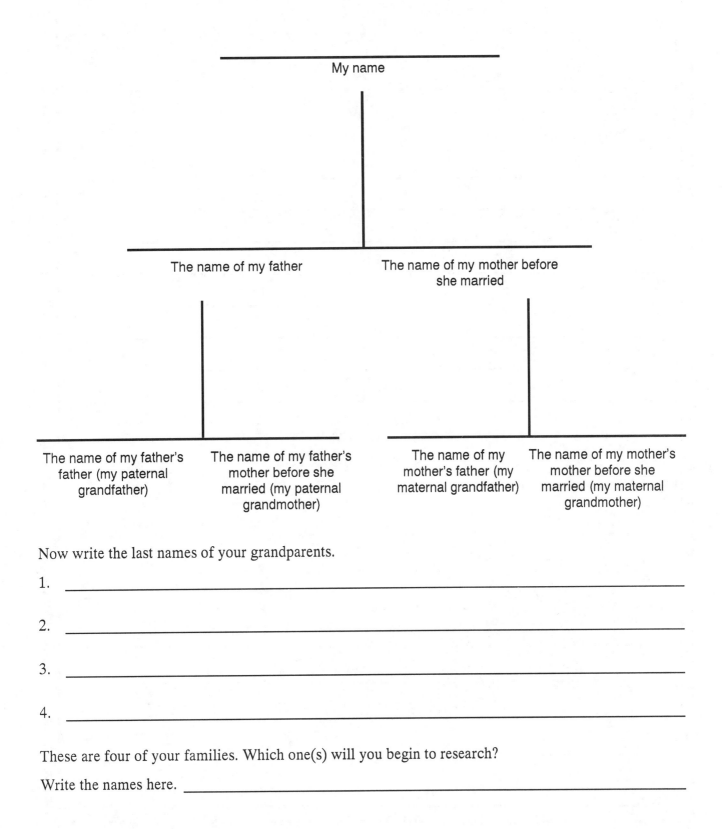

Now write the last names of your grandparents.

1. _____

2. _____

3. _____

4. _____

These are four of your families. Which one(s) will you begin to research?

Write the names here. _____

The Effect of History on Immigration

Topic _____

When _____

Brief Description

_____

_____

_____

_____

_____

_____

_____

_____

Effect on Immigration

_____

_____

_____

_____

_____

_____

_____

Venn Diagram

_____ Reasons for Moving

_____ Problems of Moving

(Check the appropriate title for your Venn diagram.)

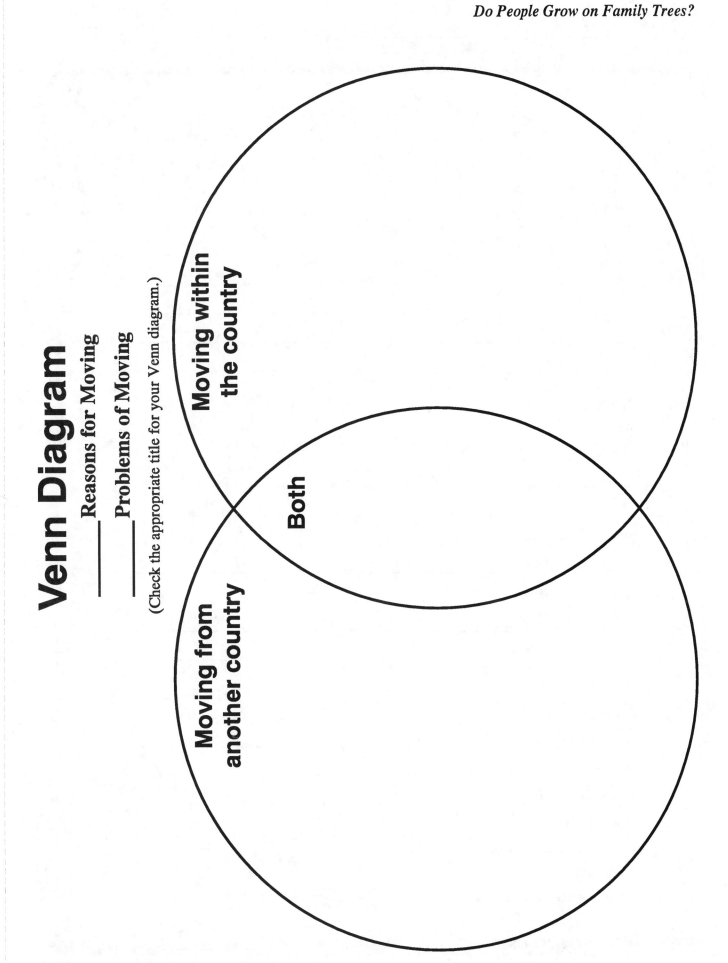

Moving within the country

Both

Moving from another country

My History

1. What is your full name? _____

    _____

2. Why were you given that name? _____

    _____

3. When were you born? _____

4. List the full names of your brothers and sisters. _____

    _____

    _____

    When and where were they born? _____

    _____

    _____

    Why were they given their names? _____

    _____

    _____

5. What is your father's full name? _____

    When was he born? _____

    Where was he born? _____

    What work does he do? _____

6. What is your mother's full name? _____

    When was she born? _____

    Where was she born? _____

    What work does she do? _____

7. When were your parents married? _____

    Where were your parents married? _____

8. Where do you live now? _____

    Where else have you lived? _____

Challenge: Make a sheet like this for your grandparents and great grandparents.

Family Group

Husband

Name _____
First   Middle   Last

Born _____
Date   Place

Married _____
Date   Place

Died _____
Date   Place

Buried _____
Place

Father's Name _____
First   Middle   Last

Mother's Name _____
First   Middle   Last

Children _____

Wife

Name _____
First   Middle   Last

Born _____
Date   Place

Married _____
Date   Place

Died _____
Date   Place

Buried _____
Place

Father's Name _____
First   Middle   Last

Mother's Name _____
First   Middle   Last

Children _____

Date: _____

Place: _____

What happened: _____

_____

_____

_____

_____

_____

_____

_____

_____

_____

_____

My Trip to America from

by

Molly's Pilgrim

by Barbara Cohen

Summary

Molly and her family immigrated to the United States from Russia. As a Jewish family they were persecuted for their beliefs. Given a homework assignment at school to bring in a doll dressed as a Pilgrim for a Thanksgiving display, Molly's mother dresses the doll as herself. When Molly protests, her mother explains that she, too, is a Pilgrim who came to America for religious freedom. She is like the Pilgrims who landed at Plymouth Rock. Molly's Pilgrim doll brings a new understanding of the true meaning of Thanksgiving.

How Many Days To America?
A Thanksgiving Story

by Eve Bunting

Summary

After a visit by soldiers to their home, a family makes the decision to leave their homeland and immigrate to America. Leaving under the cover of darkness, the wife's wedding ring and garnet necklace are used to buy passage on a small fishing boat. The mother, father, young son, and daughter, along with other passengers, overcome the hazards of the journey, including the theft of their few possessions by sea pirates. They land on American shores, appropriately enough, on Thanksgiving Day.

The outline below is a suggested plan focusing on the various activities that are presented in this unit. You should adapt the ideas to fit your own classroom situation.

Sample Plan

Day 1
- Define persecution.
- Do Who? When? Why? (page 22)
- Read the dedication in *Molly's Pilgrim*.
- Read *Molly's Pilgrim*.

Day 2
- Find out about The Statue of Liberty. (pages 51, 52, 59 & 66)
- Do a dramatic reading of "The Colossus." (page 52)
- Begin Ancestor Dolls; Homework-Questionnaires (pages 23-24)

Day 3
- Discuss the title *How Many Days to America?*
- Show the book cover; discuss the art.
- Read *How Many Days to America?*

- Write an immigration adventure. (page 21, #6)
- Do Songs of Comfort. (page 25)
- Show and divide tropical fruit. (page 21, #8)
- Continue working on Ancestor Dolls.

Day 4
- Decide what belongings to take. (page 26)
- Make a special viewing box. (page 29)
- Continue working on Ancestor Dolls.
- Compare and contrast both books. (page 28)

Day 5
- Do How They Got Here simulation. (page 27)
- Share Thanksgiving memories. (page 21, #2)
- Read other stories of immigrants. (page 21, #3)
- Have an Ancestor Doll Display.

Overview of Activities

Setting the Stage

1. What is persecution? Explain that, throughout history, people have often been mistreated because of their beliefs. It is one of the major reasons for immigration. What are other reasons for immigration? Who immigrates? Let students work with partners and complete Who? When? Why? on page 22. After each group has made a chart, create a class chart. Let each set of partners contribute some information.

2. Explain that you will soon read two books about people who immigrated to America. Ask children to listen closely and find things that are similar in the two stories.

3. Before beginning *Molly's Pilgrim* with the class read the dedication to them. How might they use their family histories (page 13) to help tell their own family stories?

4. Share *Molly's Pilgrim* with the class. If you wish to read the book aloud, allow enough time to read the book in one session.

5. When you are through reading *Molly's Pilgrim*, tell the children you will read another book about a family that comes to America called *How Many Days to America? A Thanksgiving Story*. Ask them to determine if the question in the title is ever answered in the book.

6. Before reading the book to the class, show them the cover and some of the art. Have them think about how the art will contribute to the story.

7. Read *How Many Days To America? A Thanksgiving Story*. Be sure to show the pictures as you read.

Enjoying the Books

Molly's Pilgrim

1. How would Molly's family have felt when they first saw the Statue of Liberty? Read about Lady Liberty on pages 59 and 66. Follow this up with the reading of "The Colossus" on pages 51-52.

2. Throughout the story Molly's mother speaks to her in Yiddish. She calls her, *Malkeleh* (little Molly), *shaynkeit* (pretty thing), and says she'll talk to the teacher so the *paskudnyaks* (not nice people) will stop teasing her. Most children will not recognize the Yiddish language. Yiddish developed from several languages, including German, Hebrew, Aramaic, French, and Italian. It uses the Hebrew alphabet. It became the language of the Western European Jews and, as they traveled, so did the language, borrowing from many other languages including English. It is still spoken today, but not as widely as it once was.

3. The Pilgrim doll that drew the most attention in class was Molly's. This was because it truly represented Molly's own ancestry. Give students the opportunity to make ancestor dolls (page 23). Complete this project over several days; it is an ideal homework assignment. Display the finished dolls.

4. There is little doubt that Molly's family passed through Ellis Island on their journey to America. What was it like on their arrival? Read about what might have happened to them and do the simulation on page 62.

Overview of Activities *(cont.)*

How Many Days To America? A Thanksgiving Story

5. Talk about the subtitle, *A Thanksgiving Story*. Why do students think the story was subtitled? Share the Pilgrim story on page 76.

6. Where does the family come from? Where do they land? Let your children try to answer these questions. Have them write a story about the family and their immigration adventures.

7. How are the children comforted on the trip? After reading the lines given in the story have the children complete the Songs of Comfort on page 25.

8. During the voyage in *How Many Days to America?* the family is given food to eat. The food consists of papayas, lemons, and a coconut. Bring these fruits into to show your class. Let them brainstorm ways the food could have been divided and how the coconut was opened. Let them taste these tropical fruits.

How Many Days to America?/Molly's Pilgrim

9. Molly's family probably sailed to America in steerage class and could carry only what they could hold. The family in *How Many Days To America?* brings very little with them. Let children make some decisions about what they might bring with them if they were emigrating to a new land. Have them complete Treasured Belongings on page 26.

10. Are the two books alike or different? Complete the activity on page 28 to see how your class views the pairing of these two pieces of literature.

11. What did the landing of the two families look like? How would you visualize the arrival? Let students make a special viewing box following the directions and using patterns on page 29.

Extending the Books

1. What was the trip on the boats like for the families in both books? Try the simulations on page 27 to give children a feel for what if might be like.

2. Both books have Thanksgiving in common. The subtitle for *How Many Days To America?* is *A Thanksgiving Story*. Ask children why this might be. Do they have any special memories of their own families' Thanksgivings?

3. Many other immigrant children had experiences similar to those in the two books. The book *An Ellis Island Christmas* by Maxinne Rhea Leighton (Viking, 1992) is an enchanting story of a young Polish girl and her family's immigration to the United States. This book details the voyage over on the boat which is probably most similar to Molly's. But like the narrator in *How Many Days To America?* while on the boat, the little girl is comforted by the song her mother sings to her. Choose some other titles from the bibliography (page 79) and read them with your class.

Who? When? Why?

The family in *How Many Days To America?* leaves their country immediately after soldiers come to their home. Molly's family flees a little town in Russia called Goraduk because the Cossacks (Russian soldiers) were persecuting the Jews. When Molly cries to return to her old homeland Mama comments, "If the Cossacks haven't burned it down."

Throughout history some groups of people have been treated badly because of their beliefs or principles. Often they have had to leave their homeland in order to survive. Both stories demonstrate this reason for immigration.

Persecution is only one reason people immigrate. Other reasons include famine, lack of economic opportunities, and the desire for a better education.

What other groups have immigrated to America? Why did they come? In what years did they arrive? How many people came from each country? To find the answers to these questions, do some research. Use encyclopedias and reference books. Use the information you find to fill out the chart below.

Who?	When?	How Many?	Why?
Eastern-European Jews	1880's - 1920	About 2 ½ million	Religious Persecution

Ancestor Doll

In *Molly's Pilgrim,* Molly is asked to make a doll for Thanksgiving. She knows it is different from the traditional pilgrim dolls made by the other children. It is her teacher who makes the children in the class realize that Molly's mother, as others before her, is truly a pilgrim for she too came from another country to the United States seeking religious freedom.

Like Molly, you too will make a doll. As Molly's doll represented her native Russia, so your doll will represent the country of your origins.

Before beginning your doll you will need to find out some information. Read the questions on page 24. Take them home and answer them with the help of your parents or other family members. You may find that you have more than one country to choose from. Once you have decided on the country, you may make your doll.

You will need the following materials:

- wooden clothespin or wooden spoon
- tacky glue or hot glue gun (use under adult supervision)
- stapler
- scissors
- fabric or paper scraps
- fine point markers
- yarn
- pictures of clothing from the time period of your ancestors

Using a wooden clothespin or wooden spoon, begin by drawing a face on the doll with a fine point marker. Then choose the fabric or paper that you will need to make the clothing. Select materials that represent the colors of the country. Cut out the clothing with a pair of scissors. Glue or staple onto the clothespin or spoon. Make sure to add hair. Use yarn or draw it on with a marker.

Display your doll along with the Ancestor Doll Card on page 24. A simple doll stand can be made. If you are using a clothespin, clip the pin onto the side of a small box. If you are using a wooden spoon, poke a hole in the bottom of the box, turn the box over, and put the doll into the hole to display.

Parent Questionnaire

Parents, please take time to answer these questions. When your child has the answers, he or she is to choose a country that represents his or her ancestry and create a doll. The form below should be attached to the doll.

In what country were you or your ancestors born? _____

Are there still family members in that country? _____

Why did they leave the country of their birth? _____

Who were the first members of your family to arrive here? _____

How did they get to the United States? _____

When did they arrive in this country? _____

What are or were other languages spoken by your family members? _____

Are there any celebrations or traditions that the family brought over that are still observed? _____

_____

_____

Do you have any pictures of them to share? _____

Can you share any interesting information about your family or their immigration to this country?

_____

_____

Ancestor Doll

My name is _____

My doll represents _____

Some interesting information about _____

_____

_____

_____

_____

Songs of Comfort

"Sleep and dream, tomorrow comes
And we shall all be free."

These are the words to the song that Father sings to his children in *How Many Days to America?* It is the only time the boy feels safe.

Answer these questions.

What do you think the words to the song mean? _____

_____

Why do you think the song made the boy feel safe? _____

_____

Parents often sing songs and lullabies to little children when they put them to bed. These might include classic lullabies such as the "Cradle Song (Sleep, Baby, Sleep)," "Go to Sleepy (All the Pretty Little Horses)," or "Lavender's Blue." (These can be found in *Tom Glazer's Treasury of Songs for Children,* Doubleday, 1964.)

What songs did your parents sing to you as a little child? Do you remember any words or phrases that made you feel good? Write down the titles and the words or phrases that you remember.

_____

_____

_____

_____

_____

Bring home the list that you have made. Check with your family and see if you they can help you add to it. Compare what you have written with what your family remembers. Talk about what the songs mean to you and your family. Why were these songs chosen? When were they sung—at bedtime, when you woke up, when you were ill, or when you were upset? Who sang the songs to you? Were the same songs sung to all the members of the family or did each person have a special song?

Write Your Own Song

Try writing the lyrics (words) for a song of comfort. Decide what you want to write about. Will it be a person, an animal, a place, or an experience?

Next decide who your audience will be. Will you write to comfort friends your own age, your parents, or a little child? Once you know what you want to write and who you wish to write for, try writing a short verse for a song. You may wish to choose a melody and write words that would go to it or add music to an original verse. Perform the song for your class.

Treasured Belongings

In both books the families immigrate to America. In leaving their native lands, they leave behind many of those things that are important to them. In a very short time they must make decisions about what few, small items they wish to take with them. It is your turn now to make some decisions. What would you take with you if you suddenly had to leave this country? Would it be something you would play with on the trip? Maybe it would be your favorite book. Perhaps you would choose a gift someone special gave you. Choose carefully. You may bring only five items. They must fit into a backpack. You will be responsible for carrying them.

Write your choices and your reasons for them in the chart below.

Choice	Reason

How They Got Here

The family in *How Many Days To America?* leaves suddenly after soldiers visit their home. They are able to find a boat to bring them to America. It is not a very large boat, and they need to share it with several other families. During the trip the few belongings they have are stolen. The first time they find land they are turned back. The seas are rough. Although an exact year is not given, we can assume that the family immigrates during modern times.

The family in *Molly's Pilgrim* probably came to the United States by boat. Since they came from Russia, they probably came on a large ship, perhaps in steerage class. The immigrants would be crowded into dark, smelly areas, sleeping in narrow bunk beds. They would have immigrated sometime in the late 1800's to early 1900's when Jews were persecuted in Russia.

Although at very different times in history and from different parts of the world, both families had to endure hardships. It was the lure of the opportunities the new world presented that made it all worthwhile to endure such difficult sea voyages.

What would such a journey be like? Try one of these simulations to find out.

Simulation 1

Mark off a small area on the floor (about 4' x 6'/1 m x 2 m) with masking tape. Have children wear several layers of clothing such as coats and sweaters. Let them carry a few small objects such as a book or a doll. Begin by putting a comfortable number of children into the area. Have them sit down. Tell them they may not move out of the marked off area. How does it feel? Now gradually start adding children to the area, telling them to sit down. Remind everyone they must stay within the marked lines. Ask a few children to try to take off a coat or a sweater. Have another try to turn around. As the area gets more crowded, observe what happens. When the children begin to get very restless or spill over the lines, it is time to end the simulation. Spend a few minutes asking the children how it felt to be crowed into such a small space with so many people. Would they want to spend several days on a boat doing that?

Simulation 2

For this exercise to be most effective, do it just before lunch when children are hungry. Blow up an air mattress. Put several children on it. Have the children move slowly around on the raft. Turn the lights out in the room and blow a fan on the children. Spray some water from a spray bottle on them. Tell them they cannot talk to one another. At some point tell them very sternly that you want anything of value they have with them. When you see them start to get very restless or upset, stop the simulation. Ask them if they would like to be cold and hungry and have what few possessions or little bit of money they have taken away.

Compare the Two

Molly's Pilgrim and *How Many Days to America?* both focus on stories of immigrant families. Although the families are from different parts of the world, they both immigrate to America.

How are these books different? How are they the same? To help find out the answers to these questions, use the diagram on this page. In the space marked different write what is different about the two stories and in the space marked the same write those things that the stories had in common. When you are finished, study your diagram. Were there more similarities or differences in the two stories? What conclusions can you draw about the two families based on this information provided in the diagram?

Both

Molly's Pilgrim

How Many Days to America?

28

Arrival View

Many immigrants came to the United States in boats and ships. Although a ship is not mentioned in *Molly's Pilgrim*, it is highly likely that Molly's family came to America on a large, crowded ship. Since they came from Russia, they arrived in New York.

On the other hand, the family in *How Many Days to America?* comes to America in a small, crowded boat. Their first sight of the United States was of a wooden dock, palm trees, and people calling "Welcome to America."

What did each arrival look like? Make a special viewing box that depicts one of the family's arrivals in America.

You will need:

- shoebox
- tissue paper (light blue, other light colors)
- blue construction paper
- tape or glue

- scissors
- markers, crayons, colored pencils
- patterns (page 30)
- craft knife

Directions

1. Choose which family's arrival you want to view, the one in *Molly's Pilgrim* or the one in *How Many Days to America?*

2. Use a craft knife and cut a hole about 2" (5 cm) in diameter in one end of the box. This will be the part you look through. Cut off one end of the shoe box. In the top of the shoe box, cut a rectangular hole, leaving a one inch minimum around the edge. Tape or glue light blue tissue paper over the rectangular hole in the lid. This will let light into the box.

3. Use crayons, markers, or pencils to decorate the inside of the viewing box. These should be scenes that might be seen from a shore—a sunset, or other boats, for example.

4. Glue or tape blue construction paper to the bottom of the box.

5. Trace the wave pattern on page 30 as many times as you feel you need to make waves. Fold them at the fold line. Use glue or tape and attach them to the bottom of the box.

6. Make your own patterns or use the ones provided on page 30. Choose a boat pattern that is appropriate to the story you choose. Color it, adding people if you wish. Fold on the fold line and glue this onto the "ocean floor," perhaps in between waves.

7. Add the Statue of Liberty or palm trees.

8. Tape or glue light-colored tissue paper onto the back of the box that was cut off.

9. Look through the hole. View the special scene of immigrants coming to America.

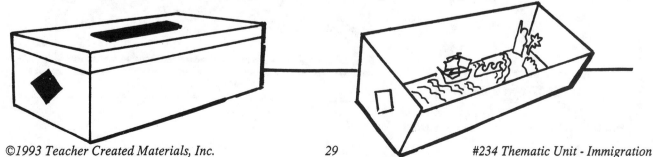

Arrival View Patterns

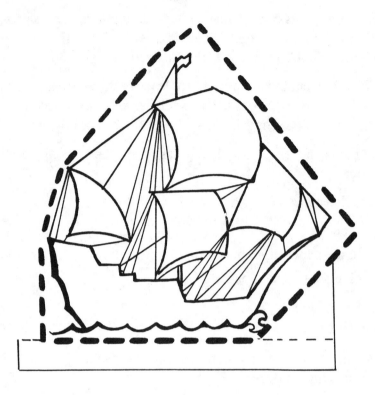

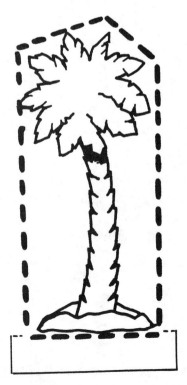

30

Hello, My Name Is Scrambled Eggs

by Jamie Gilson

Summary

What happens when Harvey Trumble, a well-meaning seventh grader from Pittsfield, Illinois, decides to Americanize a newly arrived Vietnamese immigrant? At first, Harvey thinks its all just fun and games. Within a few days, he has Tuan Nguyen eating hot dogs, playing computer games, and spouting slang. He even takes it upon himself to change Tuan's name to "Tom Winn." Then the reality of the situation begins to sink in. Harvey discovers that behind Tuan's polite smiles and calm demeanor resides the pain of having witnessed pirates murder his uncle aboard the fishing boat that was taking his family from Vietnam to Malaysia. By the end of the story, Harvey realizes that Tuan is and always will be attached to his Vietnamese heritage; and the two boys are planning to share a Thanksgiving meal together at which both pumpkin pie and pho tai will be on the menu.

The outline below is a suggested plan for using the various activities that are presented in this unit. Adapt these ideas to fit your own classroom situation.

Sample Plan

Day 1

- Read chapters 1 through 3 of *Hello, My Name Is Scrambled Eggs.*
- Begin A Newcomers Welcome Book. (page 47)
- Complete Harvey Was Here math. (page 35)
- Plan a tour of your community. (page 42)
- Discuss meanings of idioms. (page 37)

Day 2

- Read chapters 4 and 5 of *Hello, My Name Is Scrambled Eggs.*
- Continue working on A Newcomers Welcome Book (page 47)
- Learn how to use chopsticks. (page 38)
- Finish and share tour plans. (page 42)
- Play charades. (page 44)

Day 3

- Read chapters 6 and 7 of *Hello, My Name Is Scrambled Eggs.*
- Make Hello, My Name Is... name tags. (page 40)
- Practice following directions. (page 34)

- Answer questions about quotes from story. (page 43)
- Learn how to play marbles. (page 39)

Day 4

- Read chapters 8 and 9 of *Hello, My Name Is Scrambled Eggs.*
- Begin working on News Special. (page 36)
- Learn a magic trick. (page 45)
- Finish A Newcomers Welcome Book (page 47)
- Play Borrowed Words Game (page 49)

Day 5

- Read chapters 10 and 11 of *Hello, My Name Is Scrambled Eggs.*
- Continue News Special. (page 36)
- Learn the difference between similes and metaphors. (page 41)
- Practice the game of marbles. (page 39)
- Play charades. (page 44)

Overview of Activities

Setting the Stage

1. Have students find Vietnam on a world map. Discuss the possible route a boat might take to get from Vietnam to the United States. Would the boat most likely arrive at the east or west coast?

2. Share with the students some history of Vietnam and the reasons many people fled the country in the 1970's and '80's. (North Vietnam took over South Vietnam and made it a communist country. A war ravaged the country.) Use encyclopedias or other reference books to find information.

3. Direct students to begin making the Newcomers Welcome Book. In it, students will suggest places to eat and shop, things to do, emergency numbers, etc. Students may work in groups of four to six people. They may use the cover and introduction on page 47, or they may create their own. Sample pages are provided on page 48; but students should be encouraged to add more pages. Have students include phone numbers and addresses of places they recommend. This book may be given to newcomers who register their students at school or given to the Chamber of Commerce to distribute to people who inquire about the community.

4. Share some idioms with the students. Ask what they mean, then have them describe what the literal translation would mean. For example, "I'm a little hoarse today" means it is hard to talk, not I'm a small animal. The book, *The King Who Reigned* by Fred Gwynn, (Messner, 1981) illustrates idioms in a humorous manner. Use the exercise on page 37.

Enjoying the Book

1. Begin reading *Hello, My Name Is Scrambled Eggs*. The sample plan includes suggested reading for each day; adjust the amount according to your students' ability and interest levels.

2. Have students do page 35, Harvey Was Here. In order to complete this assignment, students must be able to find 20% of a number. Review percents with students. Remind them to convert the percent into a decimal and multiply it by the number.

3. Tell students to imagine that they will give someone a tour of their community (page 42). They should plan a full day of activities to last from 8:00 A.M. to 7:00 P.M. Allow time for students to share their schedules. Were there many commonalities? What was the most popular activity?

Overview of Activites *(cont.)*

Enjoying the Book *(cont.)*

4. Share the book *How My Parents Learned to Eat* by Ina Friedman (Houghton Mifflin, 1984). It is a story about an American sailor in Japan who likes a Japanese woman, but is embarrassed to eat with her because he cannot eat with chopsticks. The woman thinks he is embarrassed of her because she cannot use a fork. They both secretly learn to use the other's eating utensil.

   Have students use page 38 to learn to use chopsticks; then have them write and illustrate directions for using a fork.

5. Give students an opportunity to play charades. See page 44 for directions.

6. Let students make name tags with ways to say hello in different languages. (See page 40.) Students may use straight pins or double stick tape to fasten name tags to their clothing. You may wish to use the tags to label objects around the classroom in different languages.

7. Page 34 provides a good exercise in following directions. Direct students to read all directions carefully before beginning. The students who do read the directions will enjoy watching those who do not.

8. The quotes and questions on page 43 will allow students to relate the story to their own lives.

9. Bring in marbles or have students bring marbles to class. Learn to play marbles (page 39). Be sure the marbles are identifiable so students get their own back after playing.

10. Have students do a news special about immigration. See page 36 for directions.

Extending the Book

1. If you know any magic tricks, present them to the students to introduce the magic trick on page 45. Allow students to teach the class any magic tricks they know.

2. The Borrowed Words Game (page 49) will give students the opportunity to learn some words that were brought to the English language from other countries.

3. The exercise on page 41 will help students learn the differences between the similes and metaphors used in the book, *Hello, My Name is Scrambled Eggs.*

4. Have students use the recipe on page 73 to make some Vietnamese food. If possible, take a field trip to a Vietnamese restaurant.

Following Directions

Mr. Tandy, the math teacher, stressed the importance of following directions, which led to a misunderstanding when Tuan thought he should literally follow someone.

"Your problem," Mr. Tandy said to the class, "is that you're not reading carefully enough. You're not following directions. ...You must learn to follow directions." He chopped the air with his hand to pound out every single syllable. "Fol-low the di-rec-tions!" "Where," he (Tuan) asked Mr. Tandy, "where is...Directions...so I can follow him?"

Below you will find an exercise on following directions. Read it all before you begin the assignment.

1. Add three plus seven, then add ten to your answer.

2. Pat your head once for every stripe on the American flag.

3. Write the letters in the alphabet that come between the letters "f" and "l."

4. Balance on only one foot for five seconds.

5. Subtract eight from sixteen.

6. Write three words that end in a silent "e."

7. Ignore the first six directions.

8. Fold your hands and smile when you are finished.

Harvey Was Here

Harvey's father asked him to price some merchandise for the 20% off sale. Harvey has been known to make mistakes. (Remember the toothpaste?) Help him out by checking his work on the items below. If the item is marked correctly, put a star on the blank line under the price. If it is priced incorrectly, write the correct sale price on the blank line. The first one is done for you.

Monday Morning News Special

To present current events, the students in Ms. Ward's social studies class present a TV news program, complete with commercials, every Monday morning. Suzana gave a report about the refugees leaving Vietnam. In her report she included some reasons the people have for leaving (not enough food; fear of Communists), as well as some hardships they endure on their way to the United States (some are shot at while leaving, some get attacked by pirates on the South China Sea).

Now it is your turn to do a news special about immigration. Your report may be about current immigration or you may pretend you are able to go back in time and report on earlier immigrants. You may get your story idea from an actual news story or you may interview someone you know who is an immigrant. Be sure to include in your report the reasons the people had for leaving their homeland, the hardships endured on their way to the United States, how they got here, and how they are doing now.

You will also do a commercial that pertains, in some way, to immigration. It may be a product that would be helpful to someone just entering the country, a commercial to persuade people from other countries to move to the United States, or an actual product or accomplishment made by an immigrant (this may take some research).

Present your news specials to the class. This would be a good project to video tape or to record as a radio show.

Idioms

Before Tuan and his family arrived, Jeff Zito, the minister, talked to everyone about how to treat them. He told them not to shake hands, motion for them to come with your hand, or use sayings they will not understand, like "stick with me" or "hit the books."

These sayings are called idioms. Idioms are phrases that mean something other than the literal translation. For example, when Harvey said he would "show Tuan the ropes," he did not really mean he was going to show him some rope; he meant he would show him how things are done.

Below are several idioms commonly used in the English language. Working with a partner, use a piece of paper to write down how you would explain them to someone who is not fluent in English.

Don't let the cat out of the bag.

She's full of hot air.

He's got a big head.

Hit the road.

You're in the dog house.

Hold your horses.

I woke up on the wrong side of the bed.

She's talking out of both sides of her mouth.

It goes in one ear and out the other.

Don't spill the beans.

He has a green thumb.

She's making a mountain out of a mole hill.

I'm all ears.

I've got butterflies in my stomach.

He has a heart of gold.

Keep it under your hat.

Put a lid on it.

Let's put our heads together.

It's a drop in the bucket.

I'm all thumbs.

He has two left feet.

Keep a stiff upper lip.

He has to pay through the nose.

I have to bring home the bacon.

Don't throw out the baby with the bath water.

Chopsticks

When Tuan first came to the United States, he did not know what a fork was. He was used to eating with chopsticks. Harvey was used to eating with a fork and thought it would be difficult to eat with chopsticks. He says:

I would never had thought that using a fork could be so hard. ...And I wondered how anybody could possibly eat all those slippery little grains of rice with sticks.

Study the directions below, then try to pick up something using chopsticks. If real chopsticks and food are not available, use pencils to try to pick up objects from your desk.

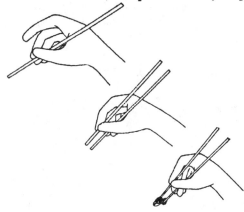

1. Place one chopstick in hand, laying stick in the V between thumb and index finger and resting it on last two fingers. This chopstick should stay still; don't let it move!

2. Use your thumb, index finger, and two middle fingers to hold the second chopstick. This chopstick will move to pick up the food.

3. Keep the bottom points of the chopsticks even. Move the second chopstick to "pinch" the food against the first chopstick. Pick up the food and eat it.

Now, in the space below, write directions and draw pictures to explain how to use a fork.

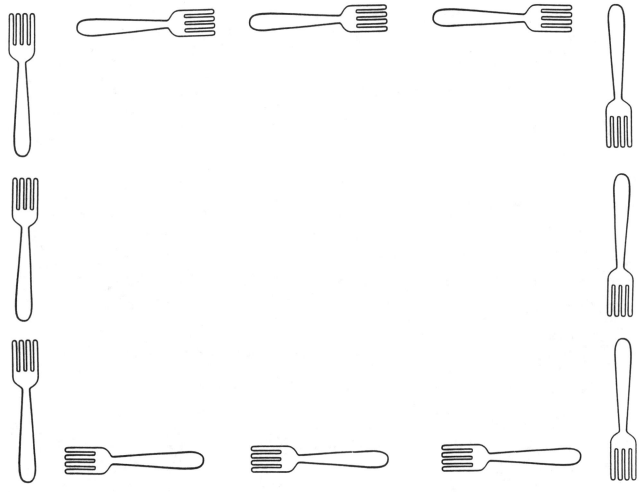

Don't Lose Your Marbles!

Tuan brought a pouch of marbles with him from Vietnam, and soon the game of marbles became very popular at his new school.

Below are directions for the standard ring game as well as the game, called the wall, that was played by Tuan and his friends. Players should decide before the game begins whether or not they will play for keeps.

The Ring Game

This game is played by drawing a large circle (about two or three feet across). This circle can be drawn with a finger in the dirt or with chalk on a flat surface. To begin, each player puts the same number of marbles (usually three to five) somewhere in the circle.

Players take turns pitching their shooters (a larger marble) from outside the circle, in an attempt to knock one of the marbles out of the circle. A player may keep any marbles he or she has knocked out of the circle. Play passes to the next person when a player fails to knock a marble outside of the ring. If a player's turn ends with his or her shooter left within the circle, the other players have an opportunity to hit it and win all the marbles won by that person so far.

The player with the most marbles when all of the marbles have been hit out of the circle is the winner.

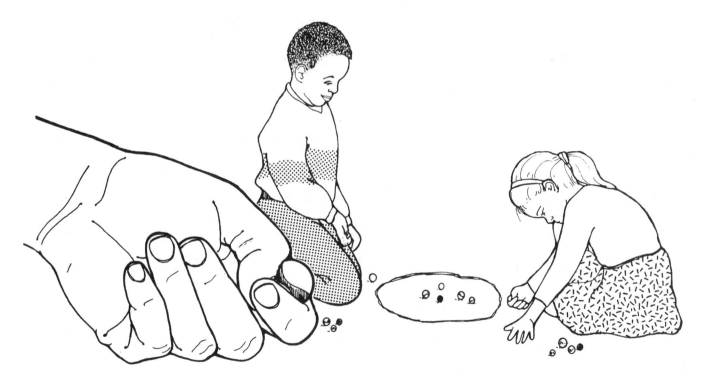

The Wall

Each player puts one marble about a foot away from a wall. Players take turns pitching their shooters off the wall, trying to hit the marbles. A player's turn continues until he or she misses. Then play passes to the next person. The player with the most marbles when all the marbles have been hit is the winner.

Hello, My Name Is...

To help Tuan learn English, Harvey uses "Hello" name tags to label practically everything in the house (including his scrambled eggs, but since they were slippery the name tag fell off).

Below you will find how hello is pronounced in many different countries. Choose a language and make a name tag for yourself. Wear the name tags in class for at least a week, so everyone can say hello in many new languages.

Extension:

Find at least three new words in the language you selected. Make name tags with your new words, and either draw a picture of what the word is or actually put the name tag on the object.

China—*ni hao ma*

Vietnam—*chao*

Japan—*konichiwa*

France—*bon jour*

Germany—*guten tag*

Italy—*ciao*

Netherland—*dag*

Brazil—*bom dia*

Commonwealth of Independent States—*preevyet*

Mexico—*hola*

Sweden—*hej*

Kenya—*jambo*

Samoa—*talofa*

Egypt—*salaam*

Poland—*dzien dobry dgen do bri*

Greece—*kalimera*

Israel—*shalom*

El Salvador—*buenos dias*

Ireland—*dia dhuit deega duht*

Armenia—*pahrev*

(Hello)	(Hello)
from	from
(country)	(country)
My name is	My name is

Similes and Metaphors

Hello, My Name Is Scrambled Eggs is made interesting both by its plot and by its use of figurative language. The story is enriched with similes and metaphors.

A simile compares things to one another by using the words *as* or *like*. It helps to better describe how something looks, feels, smells, tastes, or sounds by comparing the object to something else with which we are familiar.

Example: *But Julia looked about as scary as a piece of toast.*

A metaphor also compares two different things, but it does not use a word of comparison such as like or as.

Example: *The story problem was quicksand sucking me under.*

Listed below are examples of similes and metaphors found in *Hello, My Name Is Scrambled Eggs*. In the space provided by each example, write whether it is a simile or a metaphor.

1. _____ *The kid had this double identity like a spy.*

2. _____ *She was dancing like crazy, waving her arms like they were windshield wipers in a cloud burst.*

3. _____ *When I was there by myself, though, the stockroom was a dungeon with prisoner me hemmed in by hissing drug store serpents, rare and deadly.*

4. _____ *Quint suddenly sprang to his feet like just-popped toast.*

5. _____ *The red neckline drooped, soaking up the rivers running out of his hair.*

6. _____ *The room turned suddenly still, as if somebody had vacuumed out all the sound.*

7. _____ *My knees felt like rubber bands.*

8. _____ *I swallowed hard because my throat had become a desert.*

9. _____ *...I sprinted down the sidewalk toward the town square, parting a tide of yellow leaves."*

10. _____ *...waving and grinning like the Jolly Green Giant.*

11. _____ *A white wool shawl Mom had found for her was tucked tightly around her like a cocoon.*

12. _____ *Tom stared at the policeman as if he was a ghost.*

Challenge: Find and identify other examples of similes and metaphors from the book.

This Is Your Tour Guide Speaking

Harvey was looking forward to showing Tuan around Pittsfield.

I'd show the kid the once around town — the school, the courthouse with its fancy old stained glass, the drugstore, the cream puffs at Miles', the park where the swimming pool is, and Suicide Hill where you can skateboard when you get good.

Imagine you have an opportunity to show someone new around your town. What places would you include in your tour? Use the space below to plan a one-day tour of your town. Determine how much time you would spend at each place.

Example

8:00	Breakfast at the Coffee Cup restaurant to try the breakfast muffin
9:00	Rent a row boat to row around Lake Zurich
11:00	Visit May Whitney School
12:00	Lunch at Eng's Tea House

Tour Schedule

8:00 A.M. _____

_____

9:00 A.M. _____

_____

10:00 A.M. _____

_____

11:00 A.M. _____

_____

12:00 P.M. _____

_____

1:00 P.M. _____

_____

2:00 P.M. _____

_____

3:00 P.M. _____

_____

4:00 P.M. _____

_____

5:00 P.M. _____

_____

6:00 P.M. _____

_____

7:00 P.M. _____

_____

You Can Quote Me on That!

Write answers to the questions following the quotes below.

1. *Eric had been my best friend since I was two, but he'd moved to Pennsylvania over the summer, as far away from the middle of Illinois as Mars. Bummer.*

Do you think Harvey would have treated Tuan any differently if his friend Eric hadn't moved away? Why or why not? _____

_____

Have you ever moved or had a good friend move away? On the back of this paper, write about how you adjusted to the change.

2. *Maybe we could just forget day one. After I'd turned his name around, I'd headed him down a metal dragon's tongue, called him like he was a mongrel pup, fed him dog-meat sausages, handed him a spear to eat with instead of two sticks, choked him with a gob of ice, stolen his blue-eye marble, and, to top it off, tried to get him to spray his head with laser beams, bang-bang. There must be an easier way to turn American.*

Harvey exaggerated the events of the day. Write what Harvey was referring to in the space provided.

metal dragon's tongue _____

called him like he was a mongrel pup _____

dog-meat sausages _____

a spear to eat with _____

chocked him with a gob of ice _____

stolen his blue-eyed marble _____

laser beams _____

3. *"He's just decided to change it. The name you've got isn't right. It used to be Tuan Nguyen. But now he's going to be..."* I tossed the sounds around in my head a few times until his name turned, without any problem at all, into...*"Tom. His first name is Tom."* Mr. Saine glanced at Tuan/Tom, who smiled and nodded, but clearly understood not a word. Mr. Saine wrote down Thomas. I took a breath, and before I let it out, had the whole thing. From Nguyen to Gwen to Win, easy as that. *"Win. His full American name is Tom Win. W-I-N."* I felt like an artist painting a brand new picture.

Do you think Harvey should have changed Tuan's name? Why or why not? _____

_____

How would you feel if someone changed your name? What would you do?

_____

_____

_____

Stop the Charade

Often, when people do not speak the same language, they use motions, rather than words, to communicate.

"Shower," I said, and did a wild charade of it, jumping around and scrubbing under my arms like a monkey.

The basic idea in charades is for someone to act out in pantomime, a word (or a series of words) which an audience tries to guess. In a class, the game can be played with groups of 6-8 players. If your class is large, you can divide the class into four or five teams and have the winning team of each round play another winning group. One at a time, the players of a given team act out their words while the other members of the team try to guess the charade. Each team performs the charade in the same way and is timed. After every team has had a turn, a timekeeper announces the team who finishes in the shortest amount of time as the winner. Each person has up to two minutes to act out his or her charade.

Example:

Suppose the charade is the phrase "as flat as a pancake." Since this phrase contains five words, the student would first show five fingers to teammates (indicating five words). When the team understands this, she then holds up one finger to indicate that she will now act out the first word of her charade. One signal that is used is for the student to hold a thumb and forefinger in the air about an inch apart, indicating a small word such as "and," "the," "or," or "as." The second word "flat" can be acted out by putting the hands together horizontally or cupping the ear to show that sounds like, or rhymes with, the word being acted out. Then the actor can "show" a cat or hat. The last word can be shown by "flipping pancakes."

Suggestions:

Choose easy words at first so the students get the idea of the game. Animals, vegetables, and fruits are good examples.

Have the charades already written on pieces of paper which the students draw out of a hat, or allow them to write some for the other team.

As students get used to signals, you can try current movie titles, literature titles, idioms, geographical names, or famous people in history.

Try it with your class. It can get noisy, but it will be fun!

Magic

Magic is very important to Quint.   Some of his tricks include reaching behind a person's ear and pulling out a quarter, and finding a marble in a pocket. He even uses his magic to earn $15.00 by performing at Julia's party. Here is a magic trick to try that would even amaze Quint.

Magic Card!

Show a friend a greeting card made from a single folded piece of paper. Tell him or her you are going to cut a hole in it and climb through.

1. Cut out a small strip from the center of the card along the fold, leaving about ¹/₂ inch (1 cm) at both ends.

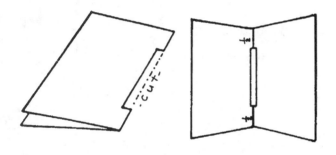

2. With the card still folded, cut lines through both halves about ¹/₂ inch apart. Stop your cuts about ¹/₂ inch from the edge.

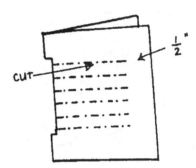

3. Turn card, and cut between each cut already made, stopping ¹/₂ inch before the folded edge.

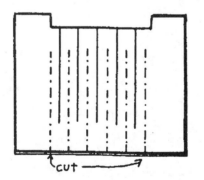

4. Carefully open card and stretch it out, pulling gently. You'll have a hole you can step through!

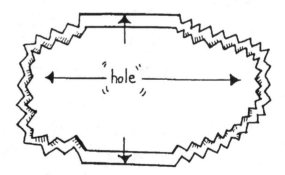

If magic interests you, check out a book of magic from your school or local library. Practice the tricks and put on a magic show! Perhaps your class can stage a magic show for another class or school assembly!

Immigration Word Bank

genealogy

indentured servant

pogrom

slave

immigration

family tree

emigration

pedigree chart

the old country

maiden name

famine

steerage

economic opportunity

ship's cabin

Ellis Island

political liberty

Statue of Liberty

ancestor

ghetto

reminisce

melting pot

prejudice

tenement

descendant

surname

reunion

patronymic

port of entry

religious freedom

Newcomers Welcome Book

Hello!

We're glad you're here. We wrote this book to welcome you to our community and to make you feel more at home. We have written suggestions of our favorite places to eat, things to do, and places to shop. We've also included some addresses and phone numbers that can be useful to you.

Sincerely,

A Survival Guide to

_____
(your town)

Welcome Book *(cont.)*

Where to Go When Not Feeling Well

Doctor:

Dentist:

Hospital:

Where to Get Information

School:

Newcomers Club:

Library:

City Hall:

Fire Department:

Police Department:

Emergency Number

Non-emergency Number

Where to Eat

Best Pizza:

Best Burgers:

Best Food:

Where to Have Fun

Movie Theaters:

Bowling Alley:

Roller Skating:

Other Places to Go:

Where to Shop

Grocery Stores:

Clothing Stores:

School Supplies:

Book Stores:

#234 Thematic Unit - Immigration　　　　48

Borrowed Words Game

Many of our words have been borrowed from other languages. This game will help students learn some of the words that have become part of the English language. To play the game, divide students into groups of eight. Each group of eight will make two teams of four. The object of the game is for team members to guess as many borrowed words as possible in a one minute time limit.

Materials:

borrowed words cards; one minute timer

Directions:

Choose one player to begin giving clues to his or her teammates. The clue-giver will tell which language the word is from, then describe the word in any way possible, including using pantomime. The only restrictions are that the clue-giver may not say something the word rhymes with or say what letter of the alphabet it begins with.

A clue-giver is allowed one free pass per turn. This should be used if the word is unfamiliar or if team members are having a difficult time guessing the word. Any additional passes will result in a point for the opposing team. After the minute is up, the team should tally and record its points, along with any point the other team has earned due to passes. Play then moves to the other team. The game continues until one team reaches 25 points or until a specified amount of time is up.

Always allow the team that went second to have last ups.

Africa tote	*Africa* yam	*Africa* goober	*Native American* moccasin
Native American canoe	*Native American* pow-wow	*Arabic* algebra	*Arabic* magazine
Arabic zero	*Australian* boomerang	*Chinese* gung ho	*Chinese* ketchup
Chinese tea	*Dutch* cruise	*Dutch* waffle	*Dutch* schooner
Dutch pickle	*Dutch* cookie	*Dutch* aardvark	*India* bandana

Borrowed Words Game (cont.)

India pajama	**India** guru	**India** shampoo	**German** kindergarten
German pretzel	**German** hamburger	**Greek** cone	**Polynesian** taboo
German poodle	**Greek** circus	**Turkish** coffee	**Greek** drama
Hebrew cinnamon	**Hebrew** camel	**Portuguese** mosquito	**French** chef
French garage	**French** ricochet	**Italian** balloon	**Italian** pasta
Italian violin	**Italian** trombone	**Hungarian** goulash	**Hungarian** paprika
Japanese tycoon	**Japanese** samurai	**French** blouse	**Spanish** plaza
Spanish cocoa	**Spanish** tomato	**Spanish** patio	**Persian** bazaar
Persian caravan	**Persian** paradise	**Malaysian** bamboo	**Malaysian** caddie

Dramatic Reading

"The New Colossus" is a poem written by a young Russian Jewish immigrant named Emma Lazarus. She wrote the poem to help raise funds for the pedestal for the Statue of Liberty. Emma Lazarus was not invited to the dedication ceremony in 1868, but her poem was finally recognized and attached to the base of the Statue of Liberty in 1903. Her poem has become world famous for focusing on the people coming to America, rather than the abstract concept of freedom.

Give students a copy of the poem (page 52) and have them read it silently. Ask if any of them can guess who or what the poem is about. If students are having trouble, emphasize the lines "A mighty woman with a torch," and "I lift my lamp beside the golden door."

Once students realize the poem is about the Statue of Liberty, share the background information about the author.

Have students read the poem dramatically. There are several ways to do this. Choose a way from the list below.

- Divide the class into groups of six to eight students. Tell students they are responsible for deciding how to present the poem. Students may all read the poem together; take turns reading one line at a time; have half the group read while the other half acts it out, etc. Allow students to be creative.

- Divide the class in half. Have the two halves take turns reading lines from the poem.

- Give students flashlights. Turn off the lights and have students shine light in the center of the ceiling as they read the poem.

- Have students take turns reading the poem one word at a time. Encourage them to pay attention so they are ready for their turns, as it will sound very choppy unless students read it quickly. This may require a bit of practice.

- Have students read one line each, standing when it is their turn to read, and remaining standing until the whole poem is finished.

- Have students read the poem facing the audience. After a student has read his or her line, he or she will turn away from the audience.

- Divide the class into three groups and have them read the poem in round. For example, the second group will begin reading the poem when the first group is on the sixth line.

"The New Colossus"

Not like the brazen giant of Greek fame,

With conquering limbs astride from land to land;

Here at our sea-washed, sunset gates shall stand

A mighty woman with a torch, whose flame

Is the imprisoned lightning, and her name

Mother of Exiles. From her beacon-hand

Glows world-wide welcome; her mild eyes command

The air-bridged harbor that twin cities frame.

"Keep, ancient lands, your storied pomp!" cries she

With silent lips. "Give me your tired, your poor,

Your huddled masses yearning to breathe free,

The wretched refuse of your teeming shore.

Send these, the homeless, tempest-tost to me.

I lift my lamp beside the golden door!"

Emma Lazarus
Jewish immigrant from Russia

Picture Prompts

Show students the pictures on pages 54-55. The first picture, "East Coast Immigration," shows a family's first sighting of the Statue of Liberty. Have students choose a person in the photo and write a journal entry describing the person's thoughts at that moment. Students should include information about where the person came from and how he/she thinks life in America will be different.

The second picture, "West Coast Immigration" shows a group of people entering the United States. Have students choose a person from the picture and write a journal entry from that person's point of view. This entry may be about why the person left his/her country, details about the trip, or where the person will go from here. Use the form below to write the journal entry.

JOURNAL

_____

_____

_____

_____

_____

_____

_____

_____

_____

_____

_____

_____

_____

_____

_____

_____

_____

East Coast Immigration
Credit: National Archives

54

West Coast Immigration
Credit: National Archives

Immigrant Statistics

An immigrant is a person who has left his or her homeland and moved to a different country to live. Immigrants have many reasons for moving from country to country. Some of the major causes of immigration are: to find better jobs; to seek a better way of life; to escape persecution, war, starvation, and/or disease.

Research the countries listed in the chart below to find out the reasons why each group came to the United States. Use the data from the chart to make a bar graph showing the number of immigrants from each country listed. Above each bar, write the years in which the group experienced the greatest wave of immigration.

Complete the questions at the bottom of the page.

Immigrants	Years of Major Immigration	Approximate Number of Immigrants
IRISH	1840's and 1850's	1 ½ million
GERMANS	1840's to 1880's	4 million
POLES	1880's to 1920's	1 million
JEWS	1880's to 1920's	2 ½ million
MEXICANS	1910's and 1920's	700,000
DOMINICANS, HAITIANS & JAMACIANS	1970's and 1980's	900,000
VIETNAMESE	1970's and 1980's	500,000

Use the data above and your bar graph to solve the following problems. You may want to use a calculator.

1. How many immigrants are represented in the chart? _____

    Round your answer to the nearest million. _____

    Use the rounded answer to complete problem 2.

2. What percent of the total number of immigrants came from each of the following groups:

    a. Poles? _____
    b. Mexicans? _____
    c. Vietnamese? _____

3. What percent of the total immigrant population represented in the chart arrived in the 1970's and 1980's? _____

Graphing Ancestry Groups

An ancestor is a person from whom another person is descended. Do you know who your ancestors are? Do they all come from the same ancestry group or do you represent more than one ancestry group?

The following chart ranks seven out of the ten largest ancestry groups in the United States and the number of people in each represented group.

ANCESTRY GROUPS IN THE UNITED STATES		
Groups	Number of People	Approximate Number of People (rounded to nearest million)
English	49,598,035	_____
Irish	40,165,702	_____
African-American	20,964,729	_____
French	12,892,246	_____
Italian	12,183,692	_____
Mexican	7,692,619	_____
Native American	6,715,819	_____

Use your math skills and the data provided on this page to complete the following tasks:

• Approximate the number of people in each group by rounding each number to the nearest million. Write the rounded numbers on the blanks in the chart.

• Use the approximations (rounded numbers) to complete the bar graph activities on page 58.

Graphing Ancestry Groups *(cont.)*

To make your graph, draw a bar for each of the seven ancestry groups represented to show the approximate (rounded) number of people from each group.

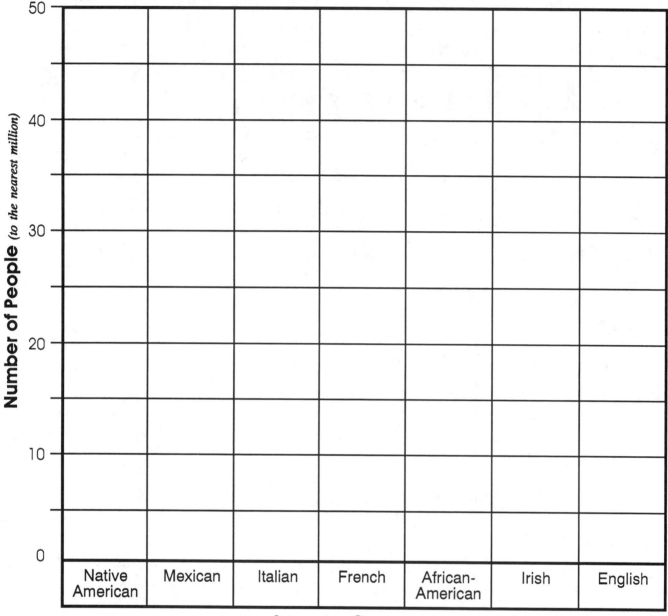

On the lines below, write four problems which require the graph information to solve. Place the solutions to each problem on the back of the page. Ask a partner or members to solve the problems. An example is given.

1. How many people are in the three smallest groups combined? _____

2. _____

3. _____

4. _____

5. _____

Statue of Liberty Math

The Statue of Liberty was a gift to the people of the United States from the people of France. It was given to the United States in 1884 and has become a symbol of the United States. The Statue of Liberty represents freedom to people all over the world. The former immigration station at Ellis Island, along with the Statue of Liberty, comprise the Statue of Liberty National Monument.

Since 1884, millions of immigrants have passed the Statue of Liberty. To many of these immigrants, it represented opportunity, the promise of a better life, and freedom.

Use the facts and measurements below to find answers to the questions at the bottom of the page.

Information	Data
statue	151 feet 1 inch (46.05 m)
pedestal	154 feet (47 m)
torch	21 feet (6.3 m)
length of hand	16 feet 5 inches (4.93 m)
length of right arm	42 feet (12.6 m)
tablet width	13 feet 7 inches (4.1 m)
tablet length	23 feet 7 inches (7.1 m)
steps in statue to torch	171
steps in pedestal	167
weight of copper skin	100 tons (90 metric tons)
weight of steel frame	125 tons (113 metric tons)
statue cost	$250,000
pedestal cost	$350,000

Questions

1. What is the total height of the statue, from the base of the pedestal to the top of the torch?

2. What is the total weight of the statue?

3. How many steps are there in the Statue of Liberty?

4. What is the area in square inches (square meters) of the tablet's surface?

5. How many inches (centimeters) taller than the statue is the pedestal?

6. What fraction of the total cost represents the cost of the statue?

7. About how many feet (meters) is it from the shoulder of the statue's raised arm to the tip of her torch?

Immigrants in Science Mini-Book

Immigrants have made many important contributions to the world. John Audubon, Alexander Graham Bell, Elizabeth Blackwell, Albert Einstein, and Jonas Salk are just a few of the many immigrants who made contributions in the field of science.

Use the pages below and on page 61 to make your own mini-book of famous immigrants in science. For each contributor, fill in the blanks with the country the person emigrated from, the contribution he or she has made to science, and one other interesting fact. Use the blank to add other famous immigrant scientists. Then, cut the pages apart and assemble into a book. Use the cover provided or design an original cover and staple together. Display the books for all to enjoy.

Immigrants in Science Mini-Book

_____

Name

John Audubon

Emigrated from _____

Contribution to science _____

Other interesting facts _____

_____

Alexander Graham Bell

Emigrated from _____

Contribution to science _____

Other interesting facts _____

_____

Immigrants in Science Mini-Book *(cont.)*

Elizabeth Blackwell

Emigrated from _____

Contribution to science _____

Other interesting facts _____

_____

Jonas Salk

Emigrated from _____

Contribution to science _____

Other interesting facts _____

_____

Albert Einstein

Emigrated from _____

Contribution to science _____

Other interesting facts _____

_____

Emigrated from _____

Contribution to science _____

Other interesting facts_____

_____

Ellis Island

Ellis Island was an immigrant processing center that was open from 1892 until 1952. During that time, over 12 million immigrants entered the United States through Ellis Island. Today, more than four out of every ten American people can trace their roots to an ancestor who entered America through Ellis Island. Built to process 5,000 new immigrants each day, it often processed twice that number.

Once the immigrants stepped off their boats, large numbered tags were tied to their clothing. They were taken to the registry hall where, after waiting in long lines, they were examined by doctors. Chalk marks were put on their clothing if any medical problems were suspected. Anyone whose clothing was marked was detained for further examination. About one out of every six people were delayed for as long as four days because of medical problems, and one out of every ten of those delayed were sent back to their homelands because the problems were judged to be serious. Those who made it past the medical examination were then questioned by a government inspector. If any answer was suspect, the person would face a board of special inquiry who would decide if the person could stay. If all tests were passed, the average stay on Ellis Island was about five hours.

Simulation

Have students reenact a group of immigrants' arrival to Ellis Island. All of the students will be immigrants, except for nine students who will play the roles mentioned below.

Have one student hand out tags with numbers to be taped to the immigrants' clothing. One student will act as the medical examiner. He or she will look in the immigrants' eyes, ears, and mouths. The medical examiner may choose about one out of every five immigrants to see the specialist. The person acting as the medical specialist will determine whether the person should be sent back or allowed to remain. The immigrants who pass the medical examination will then be sent to the government inspector. This person will choose to ask each immigrant some of the following questions:

> *What is your name?*
>
> *How old are you? Are you married?*
>
> *What is your occupation? Can you read or write?*
>
> *Where are you from?*
>
> *Where are you going in the United States? How will you get there?*
>
> *Did you pay for your passage? If not, who did?*
>
> *How much money do you have with you?*
>
> *Do you have any relatives in the United States? Names and addresses of relatives?*
>
> *Have you ever been to the United States before? When and where?*
>
> *Have you ever been in prison?*
>
> *How is your health?*

Any immigrant who seems unsure of an answer will be sent to a special inquiry board made up of five students, who will continue to ask similar questions. At the end of the questioning, they will vote to determine whether the person will be allowed to remain in the United States. Follow the simulation with a discussion.

Citizenship Test

People who apply to become United States citizens must answer 10 to 15 randomly selected questions about American history and government. Below are a few from the list of 100 possible questions. Could you pass the test?

1. What do the stripes on the American flag represent? _____

    _____

    _____

2. What country did we fight during the Revolutionary War? _____

3. What are the three branches of our government? _____

    _____

4. Who becomes president should the president and vice president die? _____

5. What did the Emancipation Proclamation do? _____

    _____

6. Who has the power to declare war? _____

7. What kind of government does the United States have? _____

8. What are the first ten amendments to the Constitution called? _____

9. Name one right guaranteed by the first amendment. _____

10. Who was the first president of the Unites States? _____

11. How many U.S. Supreme Court justices are there? _____

12. Who helped the Pilgrims in the New World? _____

13. Which countries were our enemies during World War II? _____

    _____

14. Who is the Chief Justice of the U.S. Supreme Court? _____

15. How many amendments are there to the Constitution? _____

16. How many states are there today? _____

17. What are the colors of the American flag and what does each symbolize? _____

    _____

    _____

18. What are the duties of Congress? _____

    _____

    _____

Naturalization

Naturalization is the process whereby a person from another country becomes a United States citizen.

Over the years, there have been many laws restricting immigration and naturalization. Below you will find a few of the laws. Do some research to find out the other laws and restrictions.

1790

Naturalization laws were established, but eligibility for citizenship was restricted to "free white persons."

1870

After the Civil War, citizenship was opened up to include "persons of African nativity or descent."

1943

As a gesture of goodwill towards China, who was an ally in World War II, Chinese were allowed citizenship.

1946

People of the Philippine Islands were included because of their support during World War II.

1952

The Walter-McCarran Act of 1952 was passed. Finally, "color" was removed as a criteria for citizenship eligibility and Japanese and Koreans were allowed to be United States citizens.

Working in small groups, list qualifications and rules of eligibility you think would be appropriate for people from other countries who want to become citizens of the United States. When finished, share your lists with everyone in the class. Then compare them to the actual requirements for naturalization. (See page 65.)

Rules of Eligibility

_____

_____

_____

_____

_____

Naturalization Requirements

The following are requirements for naturalization.

1. You must be at least 18 years old.

2. You must be lawfully admitted into the United States as a permanent citizen.

3. You must have lived in the United States continuously for at least five years, not counting short trips outside of the country. Also, you must have resided for at least six months in the state where you file your petition. (There are some exceptions to this requirement.)

4. You must show good moral character and believe in the principles of the Constitution of the United States.

5. You must not have been a member of the Communist Party for ten years prior to filing your application for naturalization.

6. You must not have broken any immigration laws or have been ordered to leave the United States.

7. You must be able to speak, understand, read, and write simple English, and you must be able to pass an examination about the history and government of the United States. (See page 63.)

8. You must take an oath promising to give up your foreign allegiance and any title of nobility, to obey the Constitution and laws of the United States, and to fight for the United States of America or do work of importance to the nation, if asked to.

Below is the U.S. Citizenship Petition Oath. Read it, then rewrite the paragraph in simpler words.

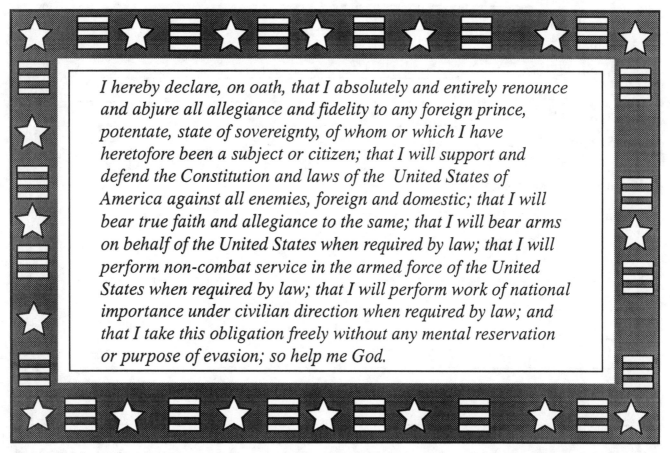

I hereby declare, on oath, that I absolutely and entirely renounce and abjure all allegiance and fidelity to any foreign prince, potentate, state of sovereignty, of whom or which I have heretofore been a subject or citizen; that I will support and defend the Constitution and laws of the United States of America against all enemies, foreign and domestic; that I will bear true faith and allegiance to the same; that I will bear arms on behalf of the United States when required by law; that I will perform non-combat service in the armed force of the United States when required by law; that I will perform work of national importance under civilian direction when required by law; and that I take this obligation freely without any mental reservation or purpose of evasion; so help me God.

The Statue of Liberty

The Statue of Liberty has always been a symbol of welcome and a promise of freedom for immigrants to the United States of America. The statue was given to the United States by the people of France in 1884. They wanted to have it ready by the Centennial in 1876, but it was delayed because France was involved in a war with Prussia. Frederic Bartholdi designed and sculpted the statue. He was sent to America to complete his plans. As he sailed into the harbor at Bedloe's Island, he knew that is where the statue should be. He decided to make the statue a lady as a symbol of liberty, and that she would face the ocean with a greeting and a promise. He decided to call it Liberty Enlightening the World. Bartholdi talked to President Grant and it was agreed that France would build the statue and the United States would build the base and pedestal.

The seven spikes in the statue's crown reach out to the seven seas and the seven continents. The seven spikes also stand for seven liberties.

1. *Civil Liberty* _____
2. *Moral Liberty* _____
3. *National Liberty* _____
4. *Natural Liberty* _____
5. *Personal Liberty* _____
6. *Political Liberty* _____
7. *Religious Liberty* _____

Discuss what you think each of these means. Next to each liberty, list what kinds of activities you can do because you enjoy this freedom.

Name the seven continents and the seven seas.

Continents	Seas
1. _____	_____
2. _____	_____
3. _____	_____
4. _____	_____
5. _____	_____
6. _____	_____
7.	_____

Fiesta Favorites

Many immigrants to the United States arrived from Mexico, over two million since the 1950's. Mexico is a country rich in tradition and, as Mexican immigrants continue to honor those traditions, they introduce many aspects of their culture into our daily lives.

You are probably familiar with piñatas, but do you know what papel picado is? You would most likely see each of these at a fiesta. Read the information below to find out about fiestas and about the origin of the piñata and papel picado. Then use the accompanying directions to make each.

Mexico celebrates many holidays, such as Independence Day on the 15th and 16th of September, and Guadalupe Day on December 12th. These and other holidays are celebrated with colorful fiestas (festivals). The fiestas usually begin before daybreak with fireworks or ringing bells. Prayer, candle burning, dancing, parades, and plenty of food are common sights at fiestas. In larger towns, fiestas are much like the carnivals or county fairs held in the United States.

The piñata game is an important part of Christmas celebrations in Mexico. Nine ceremonies, called posadas, are performed on the nine nights before Christmas to reenact the journey of Mary and Joseph to Bethlehem. Following the posadas, Mexican children play the piñata game. Although piñatas are readily available and sold in stores or made by hand in the United States today, they were traditionally handmade using earthenware or papier-mâché. The piñata is filled with candy, toys, or fruit. A piñata is often shaped like an animal. It is hung over the heads of blindfolded children who take turns hitting it with a stick until the piñata breaks, scattering the "treasure."

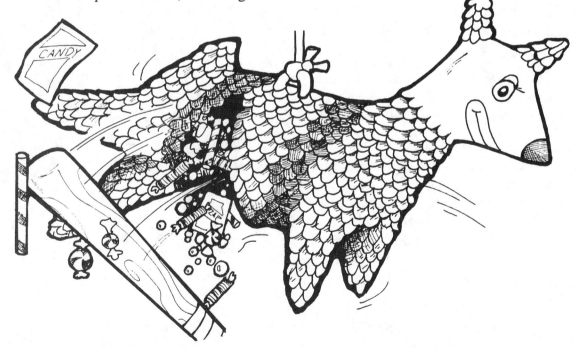

Making piñatas can be rather involved and can take quite awhile to finish. However, by using the materials and directions on page 68, you can make, decorate, and fill your own piñata in no time at all.

At the fiestas, people make and display decorations of flowers and colored tissue paper. One type of tissue paper decoration is papel picado, which is the Spanish term for "pierced paper." In addition to its use at the fiesta, papel picado is often used to decorate shops and homes in Mexico. The artist uses several layers of tissue paper and special instruments to punch designs in it. You can create a simple papel picado decoration by following the directions on page 69. You may want to hang several of these around the classroom for special celebrations.

Fiesta Favorites *(cont)*

Easy-to-Make Piñatas

Materials

- hole punch
- large brown paper bag (A grocery bag works well.)
- scissors
- brightly colored tissue paper (Try to use a variety of colors.)
- heavy yarn or string
- glue
- ruler
- candy or small prizes

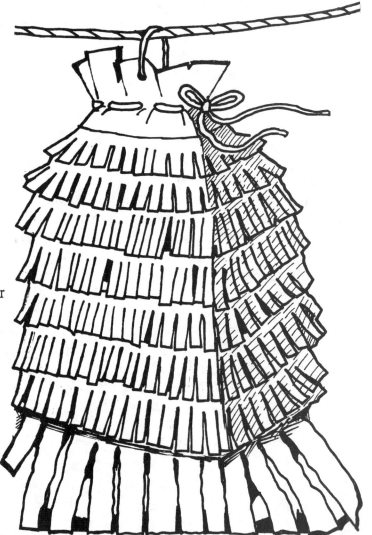

Directions

Cut the tissue paper into 4" (10 cm) strips. (If you place several sheets of tissue one on top of the other and fold in half twice, you can cut more strips at a time. Use a sturdy pair of scissors.)

Next, fringe the tissue strips by making many cuts along the edge of the strips. Be sure to leave a 1" (2.54 cm) uncut edge at the top of the strips.

Glue a tissue strip around the outside of paper bag, starting at the bottom of one side of the bag and continuing around each side until you meet the place where you began. Cut the tissue and start a new layer. Position the next strip so the fringe hangs down and covers the glued area of the first layer. Glue this next strip around the bag as you did the first. Continue adding each layer until you reach the top of the bag.

Use the hole punch to punch holes about 2" (5 cm) apart around the top of the bag. Weave the yarn or string through the holes, as shown in the picture. Next, fill the piñata with candy or prizes, pull the string or yarn so the bag is closed tightly, and secure it with a knot.

Glue colorful streamers to the bottom of the bag for an more festive look! Hang your piñata in a place where you can play the piñata game. Blindfold the players and have each, in turn, hit the piñata with a yardstick or rolled up newspaper until it is broken and all the goodies fall out. Enjoy!

68

Fiesta Favorites *(cont.)*

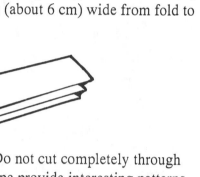

Pierced Paper Decorations

Materials

- scissors (You will need a sturdy pair of sharp scissors.)
- heavy yarn or string (for hanging decorations)
- one or more sheets of brightly colored tissue paper
- glue
- paper towel rolls

Directions

1. Cut a sheet of tissue paper into a 12" x 20" (about 30 cm x 50 cm) rectangle. Fold the sheet in half, lengthwise, several times, until you have a strip about 2 or 3 inches (about 6 cm) wide from fold to fold.

2. Keeping the tissue folded, cut out designs along the folded edges. Do not cut completely through from one folded side to the other. Designs that are geometric in shape provide interesting patterns when the tissue is unfolded.

3. When you have finished cutting out the patterns you wish to use, open the paper picado by gently unfolding it. Glue one end (width) of the tissue around the paper towel roll. Slide a piece of string or yarn (which has been attached to a wall or ceiling) through the paper towel roll and let the rest of the pierced paper hang down. Attach several other paper picado decorations to the yarn or string in the same way and enjoy your colorful display.

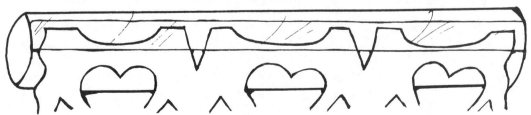

You can also use your pierced paper decorations in other ways. Simply cut out the patterns using the directions above, but do not glue the tissue to the paper towel roll. Try gluing the tissue to construction paper and use it for making placemats, window decorations, or cards. What other decorative uses can you think of?

Spool Roller Prints

Decorate your own cards using the materials and directions on this page. Use the decorated pieces of paper to prepare cards welcoming an immigrant to the area, a new student to your school, or members of your family, school, or community to a classroom activity involving your immigration unit.

Materials

- one large empty thread spool
- one pencil, thin wooden dowel, or knitting needle (Choose an item with a diameter that will allow it to fit through the center hole of the spool.)
- non-hardening clay
- one craft stick or sharpened pencil
- one old baking tray or styrofoam meat tray
- construction paper or index paper cut to desired size
- poster paints
- scissors
- soap, water, and paper towels for clean-up

Directions

Prepare your roller by first covering the surface of the empty spool with about ½" (about 1.5 cm) layer of clay. Smooth the surface of the clay as much as possible and check to see if the clay is approximately the same thickness all around.

Next, push the item you will use for your roller through the center hole in the spool.

Decide on a pattern you would like to print. You may want to design it on paper first, using words or decorations that symbolize a family or country's tradition. Press the patterns you have chosen into the clay using the sharpened end of a pencil or a craft stick. (For finer impressions you could use the end of a paper clip or a straight pin.)

Pour poster paint into the baking tray or styrofoam meat tray. Hold the ends of the spool roller and roll it back and forth across the paint until the entire clay surface of the spool roller is covered with paint.

To create a design on the construction paper or index paper, hold the ends of the roller and push it across the paper in the area where you want your design. For welcome cards, try a border design.

To use more than one print color on a piece of paper, wash the paint off the roller with soap and water and pat it dry with a paper towel before each new color. Wait until one paint is dry before adding another.

Picture This!

As you read *Molly's Pilgrim, How Many Days to America?*, and *Hello, My Name Is Scrambled Eggs*, did you notice any similarities or differences in the way these books were illustrated?

Illustrators and artists often use a specific technique or art material(s) to create to a certain mood for the story. The art becomes an important part of the story.

Use two copies of the sketch below. On the first sketch color the illustration by using pastel chalks. Use charcoal to color the second copy of the sketch.

Compare the two sketches. Consider which you like better and why. Do the two pictures create a different mood? In what way(s)?

Decorated Bowls

Many immigrants who come to the United States bring with them treasured items from their native countries. The colors, decorations, shapes, or figures that adorn these objects often symbolize an important part of the history or tradition of the land from which the people emigrated.

Choose one of the countries represented in this unit, or a country from which some of your ancestors emigrated. Research the art, culture, celebrations, etc., to find a meaningful decoration that you can use. Then make a papier-mâché bowl using the directions below. When you are done, paint and decorate it to represent the country you have chosen. The bowls can be used during the culminating activity for serving such things as bread, chips, or other dry foods.

Materials

- one bowl (for use as a mold)
- one bowl (for making papier-mâché mixture)
- newspaper (Supply enough to cover working area and for making papier-mâché strips.)
- tempera paints
- paint brushes
- flour
- water
- measuring cups
- mixing spoon
- petroleum jelly
- acrylic finish (to be used as a sealer)

Directions

Cover working area with some of the newspaper. Turn the bowl you will be using as a mold upside down and cover it with petroleum jelly. This makes removal of the finished papier-mâché bowl easier. Tear newspaper into 1" x 4" (2.54 cm x 10 cm) strips, enough to cover the bowl's outer surface and the rim.

Prepare the glue mixture in a bowl by adding one cup (250 mL) flour to one cup water. Double or triple the recipe as needed.

Dip a newspaper strip in the glue mixture, lift it out gently, and allow it to drip some of the excess glue back into the glue bowl. Do the same with each strip you add to the bowl you are making.

Cover the outside surface of the bowl with a vertical layer of newspaper strips; then, apply a second layer of strips horizontally. Continue adding layers in this way until about five layers have been applied.

When the papier mâché bowl has dried, pry it from the bowl you used as the mold. Paint the bowl with tempera using the design you chose. Add one or two coats of acrylic sealer.

Although you cannot wash the bowl, it can be wiped clean.

72

World Class Recipes

Immigrants have brought with them a bounty of foods from all over the world. Prepare and share a variety of recipes from the countries representing their ancestry groups. Provide classroom resources for students to find out more about the foods unique to the immigrant groups in this unit.

The following recipes represent food from tropical islands, Vietnam, and Russia.

Fruit Salad Supreme

You can be creative in preparing this salad, but try to include those fruits which will give it that tropical flavor! Fill a large bowl with bite-sized chunks of the following fruits: pineapple, kiwi, banana, coconut, papaya, strawberries, honeydew, cantaloupe, and/or watermelon. Where possible and available, use fresh fruits. Mix the fruits in the bowl and serve in small paper bowls. Add the dressing below, or enjoy your Fruit Salad Supreme without a topping or with whipped cream.

Tropical Dressing

In a small bowl, mix 2 tablespoons (30 mL) each of the following ingredients: strained lemon juice, lime juice, orange juice. Add $\frac{1}{3}$ cup (80 mL) water and $\frac{2}{3}$ cups (160 mL) sugar and stir mixture. Double or triple recipe as needed.

Chicken with Mushrooms, Baby Corn, and Snow Peas

- 1 cup (250 mL) raw chicken strips
- 1 cup (250 mL) coarsely sliced mushrooms
- 1 cup (250 mL) fresh or canned baby corn
- 3 tablespoons (45 mL) oil
- $\frac{1}{2}$ pound (225 g) snow peas
- 1 tablespoon (15 mL) soy sauce
- 2 tablespoons (30mL) chopped onion
- dash of pepper

Cut chicken into 1" x 2" (2.5 cm x 5 cm) strips. Heat skillet or other large pan and add oil. (Oil heats fast and can burn. This should be done by the teacher.) Sauté onions for about 3 minutes. Add chicken and saute for about 10 minutes. Add mushrooms. Sauté for 10 minutes. Add snow peas and saute for 5 minutes. Snow peas should appear cooked but not soft. Add soy sauce and pepper for seasoning. Serve with noodles or rice if desired. Makes 6 servings.

Grandma Coan's Beet Borscht

- 1 hardboiled egg, chopped
- 1 pint (500 mL) sour cream
- 1 jar prepared borscht
- 1 small onion, grated
- 1 - 16 oz. (500 mL) can julienne beets
- salt, pepper, sugar, if needed

Gradually add sour cream to prepared borscht. Drain off $\frac{1}{2}$ can beet juice. Add beets and onion to borscht. Add the $\frac{1}{2}$ can beet juice. Add salt, pepper, and sugar to taste. Garnish with chopped egg.

Music Migrated, Too!

As immigrants traveled to new lands they brought with them the musical traditions of their homelands. Some of these traditions remained intact in the new country, but others were combined, modified, and then exported around the world only to return, modified again. Below are some examples to share with your class.

Italian Opera

Modern opera began in Italy in the late 1500's. By the end of the 1600's, it had spread throughout Europe and from there to America by way of European immigrants. Introduce your students to opera through *Aida*, one of the most popular operas of all time. In *Aida*, Italian composer Giuseppe Verdi (1813-1901) tells the story of an Ethiopian princess who was captured and forced into slavery by the Egyptians.

Leontyne Price, renowned African-American opera singer, is known throughout the world for her exemplary portrayal of Aida. She has retold the story of the opera in a beautifully illustrated book for children, *Aida* (HBJ, 1990). Read the book to students beginning with Ms. Price's "Storyteller's Notes" found at the end. Then play selected portions of a tape of the opera. A recording of Giuseppe Verdi's *Aida* (1971), conducted by Leinsdorf, with Leontyne Price, Plàcido Domingo, Grace Bumbry, and Sherrill Milnes, is available through Classical Recordings Department, RCA Victor Red Seal.

Russian Symphonies

Russian immigrants in the 1900's brought with them a strong, classical musical tradition. One of the major Russian composers of this period was Sergei Sergeyevich Prokofiev, who lived in New York City from 1918 to 1923. His classic symphonic fairy tale, *Peter and the Wolf* (1936) is beloved by children and adults alike the world over. Introduce the symphonic form to your students by using one of the many book/tape combinations, for example, *Peter and the Wolf* by Sergei Prokofiev, illustrated by Jorg Muller (Knopf, 1986).

Caribbean Calypso

The musical style of calypso originated on the island of Trinidad in the Caribbean Sea before 1830 during singing competitions held by African slaves during carnivals. It is a combination of the music of several heritages—African, Spanish, and American rhythm and blues. After 1920 this style became widely known around the world. Later it was popularized in the United States with such songs as "Day-O," "Banana Boat Song," and "Mary Ann." Appeal to record-collecting parents and grandparents for recordings of these songs or call a local oldies radio station with your request. When you play them in class, let students keep beat with the rhythm using homemade or commercial rhythm instruments.

God Bless America

One of the most popular patriotic songs in the history of the United States, "God Bless America," was composed by a Russian immigrant, Irving Berlin. Mr. Berlin wrote this song in 1918. It was not until 1938 when singer Kate Smith performed it on the radio on Armistice Day (now Veterans Day) that it became popular. As a way to say thank you to his adopted country, Irving Berlin donated the money he made fron the song to the Boy Scouts and Girl Scouts of America.

A Heritage Thanksgiving

As a culminating activity for your unit on immigration have a Thanksgiving celebration. Combine both the historical aspects of the traditional Thanksgiving with elements that students have learned about during their studies.

Begin with a review of the books *How Many Days To America?*, *Molly's Pilgrim*, and *Hello My Name Is Scrambled Eggs*. Why is Thanksgiving important to each of the books? How does it play a part in each story? What time of year must they all take place if Thanksgiving is part of each of them? Encourage students to draw comparisons among the three stories.

- Review the traditional history of Thanksgiving. See page 76 for a brief version. Ask students how Thanksgiving is celebrated in their homes. Explain that you are going to have a celebration in your classroom. It will be a Heritage Thanksgiving because it will celebrate and give thanks for the varied heritages that students' families have brought to this country.

- Invite parents and friends. Make special invitations. Use the spool roller prints on page 70 to create borders on your invitations. In your invitation you may ask parents to bring a dish to share that would reflect their heritage. You may also ask them to include a copy of the recipe so that students can share it with others.

- Before the big event, set up your classroom. Prepare various displays. These should reflect the immigration unit. Include the family trees students have made (page 13), their family history booklets (page 12), and their ancestor dolls (page 23).

- You might also have a chopstick and fork center. Put out several forks and pairs of chopsticks and some small items to pick up. Post directions on how to use chopsticks and the children's written directions on how to use forks (page 38). Encourage parents to try them.

- Decorate your room using the papel picado (page 69).

- Have children greet their guests at the door. Give each a Hello, My Name Is name tag (page 40).

- Welcome parents and guests. Explain why you are holding a special heritage Thanksgiving. Let the children talk about the books you have read, and how each book deals with immigrants and Thanksgiving.

- Provide entertainment. Children can perform the poem "The New Colossus." The poem and various ways of performing it can be found on pages 51 and 52. Let children choose which method they would like to use in their presentation. Perhaps it could be done a few different ways by different groups of students.

- Serve refreshments. Food brings people together. If parents bring food, a fun way to share is to have them label it with the name of the dish, the ingredients and the country it represents. You could also prepare the recipes found in this book (page 73). Set the table using the decorated bowls (page 72).

The Pilgrim Story

The Pilgrims lived in England where there was much religious persecution. King James would not allow them to attend the church of their choice. The Pilgrims decided to leave England to find a place where they could worship God in their own way. The Pilgrims set sail for Amsterdam and finally settled in Leiden, Holland in 1609. They were welcomed in Holland but soon realized they could not stay in Holland unless they were willing to give up their English customs and language. They decided to set sail for North America where they could establish their own community and keep the English language.

After much difficulty, they financed two small ships; the *Speedwell* and the *Mayflower*. They began their journey across the Atlantic Ocean. The *Speedwell* developed a leak and both ships had to return to port. On September 6, 1620, the *Mayflower* set sail alone with 102 people aboard.

It was a difficult voyage for the Pilgrims. Food was scarce and consisted mostly of salted meat and dry biscuits. They could not build fires for cooking or heat because the ship might burn.

The ship was only 90 feet long. People were very crowded. Many became ill due to poor conditions. One happy event did take place during the voyage. A baby was born to the Hopkins family and named Oceanus. Land was sighted on November 11. Almost three weeks later they dropped anchor and began building a settlement near what is now Provincetown, Massachusetts. Before leaving the ship, all of the men signed the Mayflower Compact which was an agreement to the fact that they were still loyal to the king of England, but would set their own laws to provide for their general good and welfare.

The first winter was difficult. There was little food, and shelters provided little protection from the cold. The Pilgrims made friends with the Native Americans who taught them to build stronger houses and how to hunt for food. When spring arrived, the Pilgrims began plowing the land and planting seeds which they carried from England. A Native American, named Squanto, became a very good friend who taught them new ways of planting and gathering food.

When the harvest came, there was plenty of food to store for the next winter. The Pilgrims were so thankful that they decided to invite their Native American friends for a feast of thanksgiving.

On the day of the feast, the Pilgrims covered the tables with food. The Native Americans brought wild turkeys, game, and shellfish. This first Thanksgiving was a joyful occasion of sharing. It was a time of games and eating that lasted three days.

Today, Thanksgiving is a legal holiday celebrated on the fourth Thursday of November.

Bulletin Board

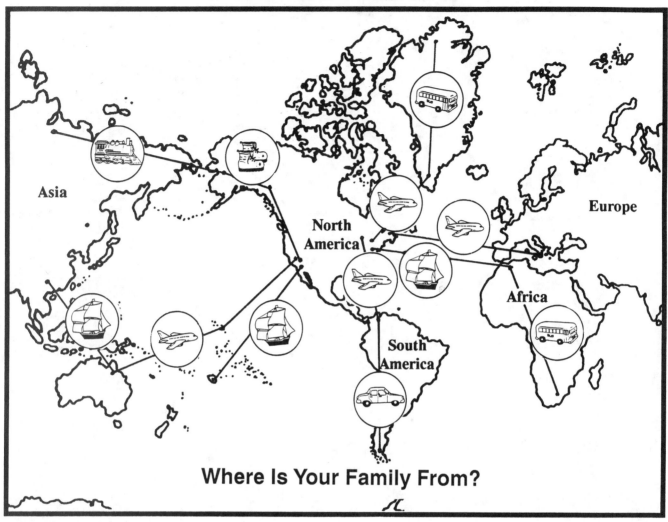

Where Is Your Family From?

Materials:

- Large world map with Western Hemisphere in middle
- Pushpins
- String
- Transportation Patterns (duplicated from page 78)
- Lettering for Title

Procedure:

1. Post map and title, "Where Is Your Family From?"

2. As students report where they or their ancestors came from, put a pushpin in that location on the map. Also put a pushpin at the point of entry into the United States.

3. Connect the two pins with string. Some students may have more than one set of pins and string.

4. Have students select from the transportation patterns, the means of transportation used to arrive in the United States. They should write their names and the names of the immigrants, if known, on the vehicles and attach them somewhere along the appropriate strings.

Transportation Patterns

Bibliography

Anno, Mitsomasa. *Anno's Journey* (Putnam Publishing Group, 1981)

Bresnick, Perry. *Leaving for America* (Children's Book Press, 1992)

Fisher, Leonard. *Ellis Island Gateway to the American Dream* (Holiday, 1986)

Freedman, Russell. *Immigrant Kids* (Scholastic, 1992)

Friedman, Ina. *How My Parents Learned to Eat* (Houghton & Mifflin, 1987)

Gilson, Jamie. *Hello, My Name is Scrambled Eggs* (Pocket Books, 1991)

Handforth, Thomas. *Mei Li China* (Doubleday, 1955)

In America...series highlights reasons for immigration and contributions to America. There are 35 cultures discussed. Some are:

Kunz, Viginia. *The French in America* (Lerner Pubns.)

Eubank, Nancy. *The Russians in America* (Lerner Pubns.)

Rutledge, Paul. *The Vietnamese in America.* (Lerner Pubns., 1987)

Patterson, Wayne, and Kim, Hyung-Chan. *The Koreans in America.* Lerner Pubns., 1977)

Kroll, Steven. *Oh, What a Thanksgiving* (Scholastic, 1988)

Kroll, Steven. *Mary McLean and the St. Patrick's Day Parade* (Scholastic, 1991)

Langley, A. & Butterfield, M. *People* (Gareth Stevens Inc., 1989)

LeVine, Ellen. *I Hate English* (Scholastic Inc., 1989)

Lewin, Hugh. *Jafta* (Lerner Publications, 1989)

Miller, Arthur. "Grandpa and the Statue" Journeys Series: *Banner* (HBJ, 1982)

Miller, Natalie. *The Story of the Statue of Liberty* (Childrens, 1965)

Payne, Elizabeth. *Meet the Pilgrim Fathers* (Random House, 1966)

Payne, Elizabeth. *Meet the North American Indians* (Random House, 1965)

Rowland, Della. *A World of Shoes* (Contemporary Books, Inc.,1989)

Sandin, Joan. *The Long Way to a New Land* (Harper & Row, 1981)

Shalant, Phyllis. *Look What We've Brought You from Vietnam* (S & S Trade, 1988)

Shapiro, Mary. *How They Built the Statue of Liberty* (Random House)

Spier, Peter. *People* (Doubleday, 1980)

Stanek, Muriel. *We Came from Vietnam* (A. Whitman & Company, 1985)

Stanek, Muriel. *I Speak English for My Mom* (A. Whitman, 1989)

Tayor, Theodore. *The Cay* (Avon, 1987)

Waters, Kate. *Sarah Morton, A Day in the Life of a Pilgrim Girl* (Scholastic, 1991)

Yarbrough, Camille. *Cornrows* (Putnam Publishing Group, 1992)

Yolen, Jane. *The Devil's Arithmetic* (Puffin Books, 1990)

Answer Key

page 35

1. ★
2. $2.72
3. ★
4. ★
5. ★
6. 32 ¢
7. $1.44
8. $2.00

page 41

1. simile
2. simile
3. metaphor
4. simile
5. metaphor
6. simile
7. simile
8. metaphor
9. metaphor
10. simile
11. simile
12. simile

page 43

1. Accept reasonable answers
2. escalator, motioned with his hand, hot dog, fork, iced tea, Tuan's lost marble, hair dryer
3. Accept reasonable answers

page 56

1. 11, 100, 000; 11, 000, 000
2. a. 9%
   b. 6.4% (or 6%)
   c. 4.5% (or 5%)
3. 9%

page 58

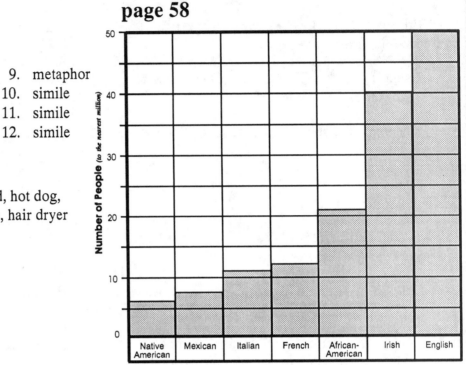

page 59

1. 305' 1" (92.99 m)
2. 225 tons (203 metric tons)
3. 338
4. 46, 129 sq. in. (29 sq. cm)
5. 2' 2" (95 cm)
6. $5/12$
7. 80' (24 m)

page 63

1. They represent the 13 original colonies.
2. England
3. Legislative, Executive, and Judiciary
4. Speaker of the House of Representatives
5. Freed many slaves
6. The Congress
7. A democratic form of government (or, a Republic)
8. The Bill of Rights
9. Freedom of speech/press/religion; peaceable assembly
10. George Washington
11. Nine
12. Native Americans
13. Germany, Italy, and Japan
14. William Rehnquist
15. 26
16. 50
17. Red stands for courage, white stands for truth, and blue stands for justice.
18. To make laws